Big Activity Book for Kids

SHEBA BLAKE PUBLISHING CORP.
BROOKLYN NY

FIND THE RIGHT WAY

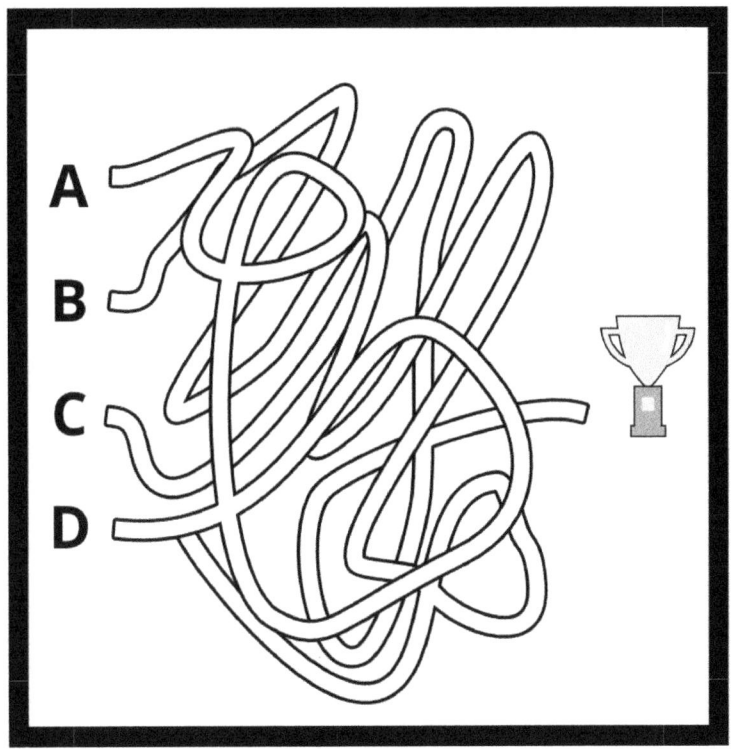

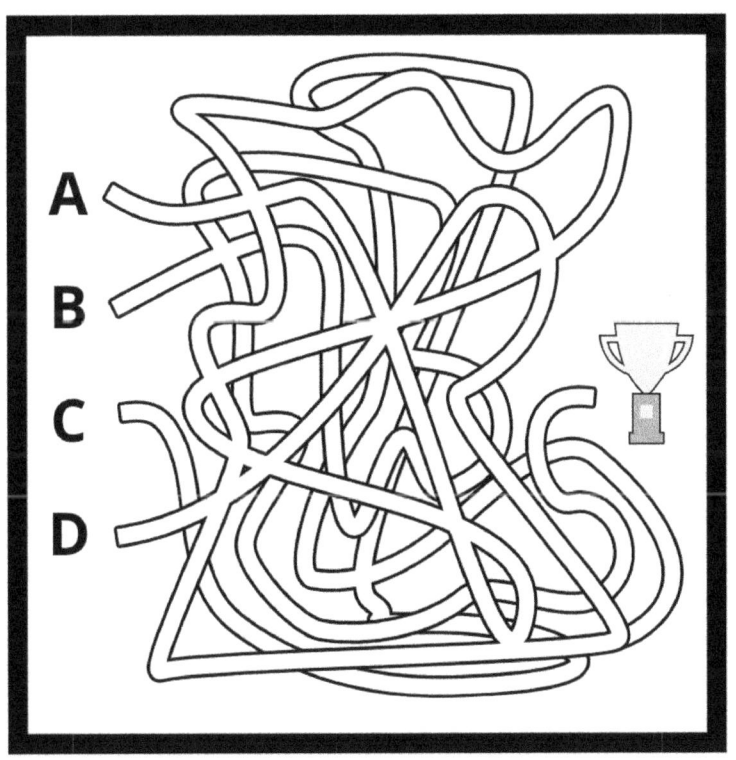

SOLUTION

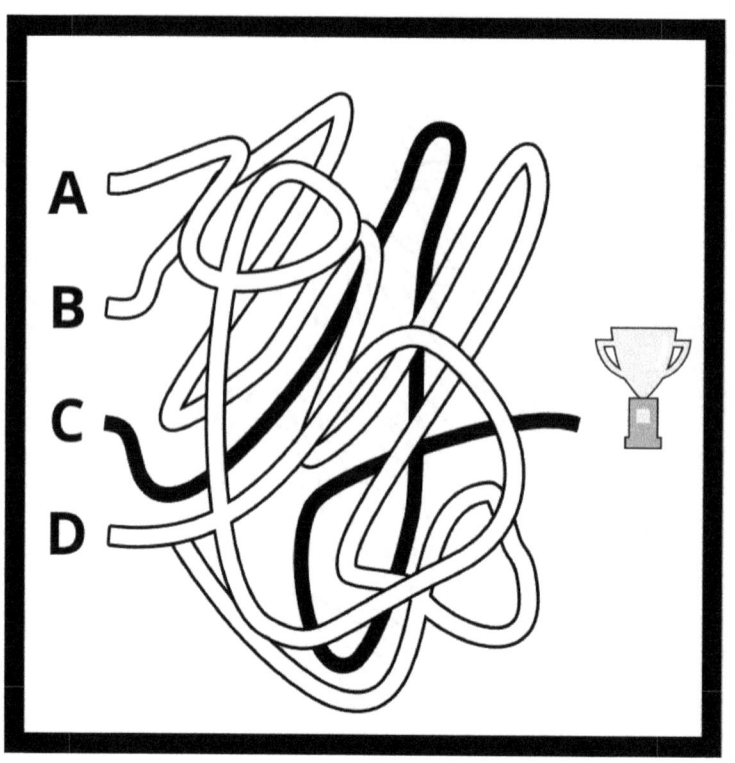

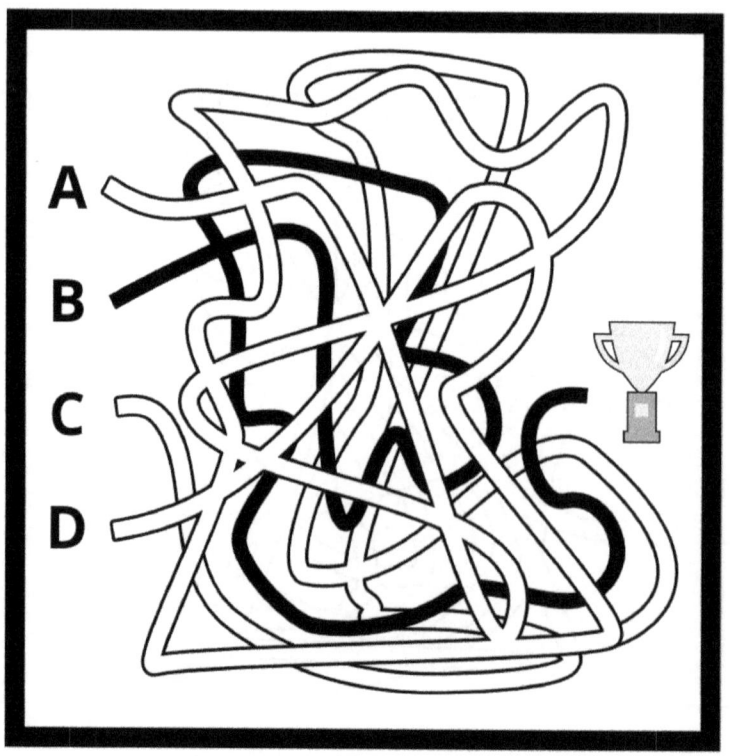

FIND THE RIGHT WAY

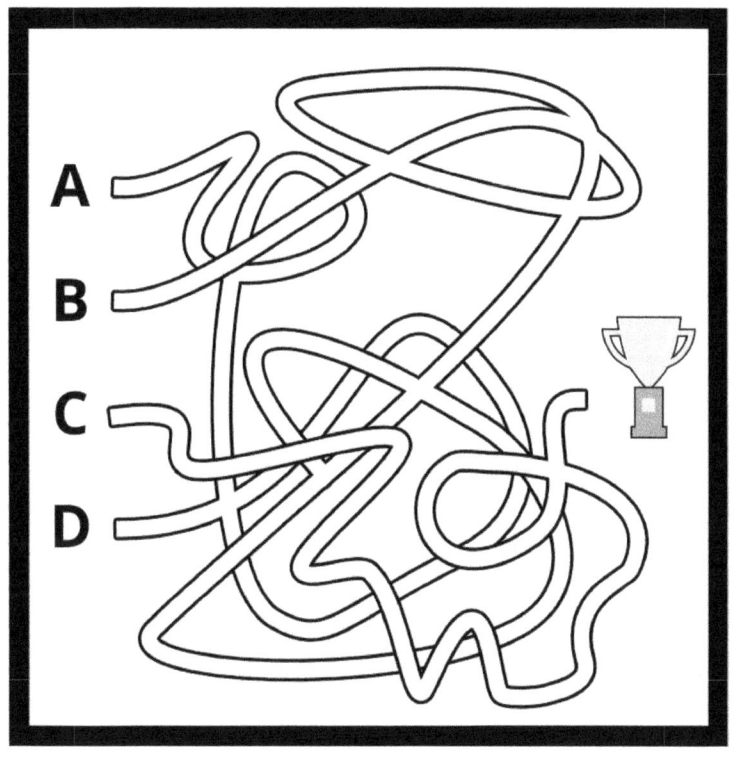

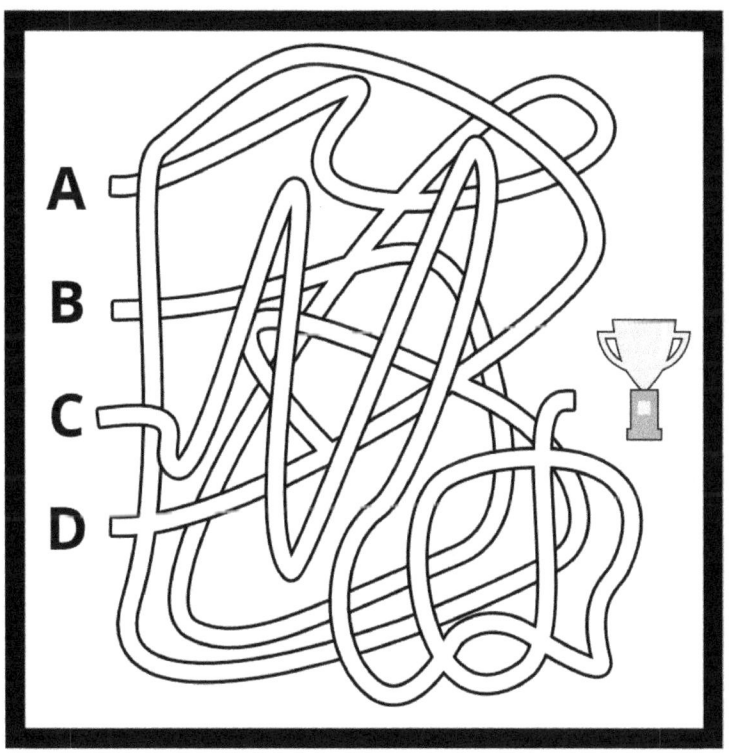

SOLUTION

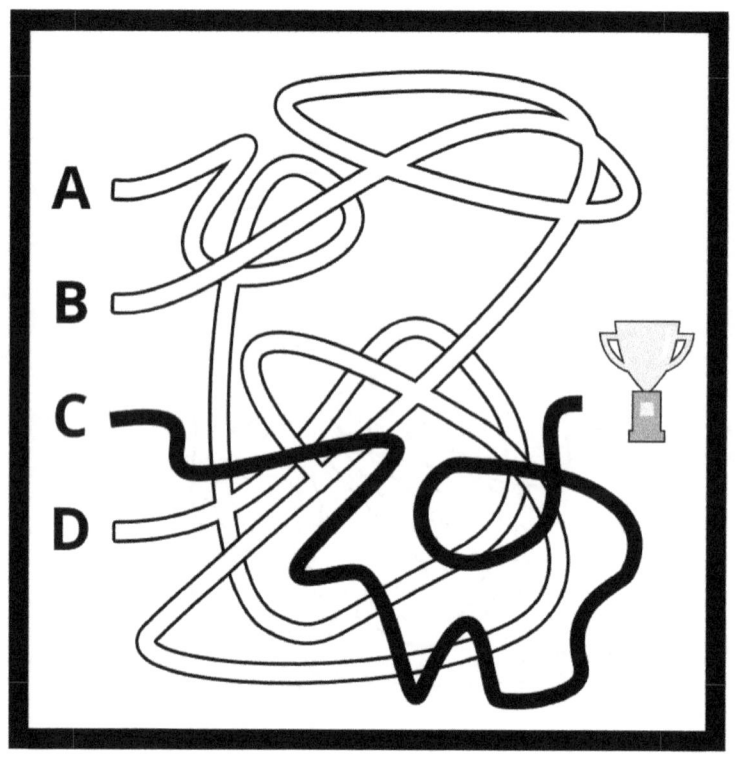

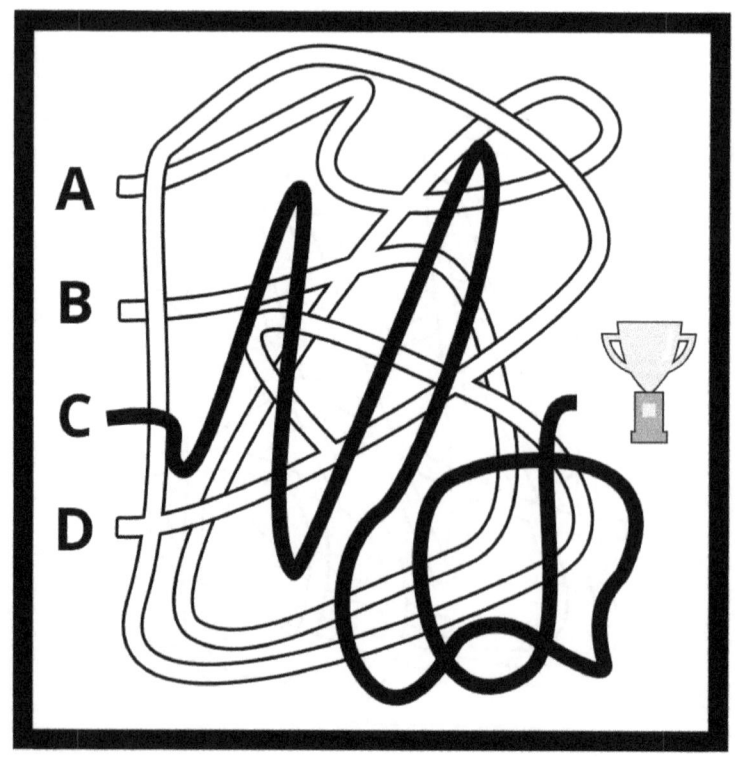

FIND THE RIGHT WAY

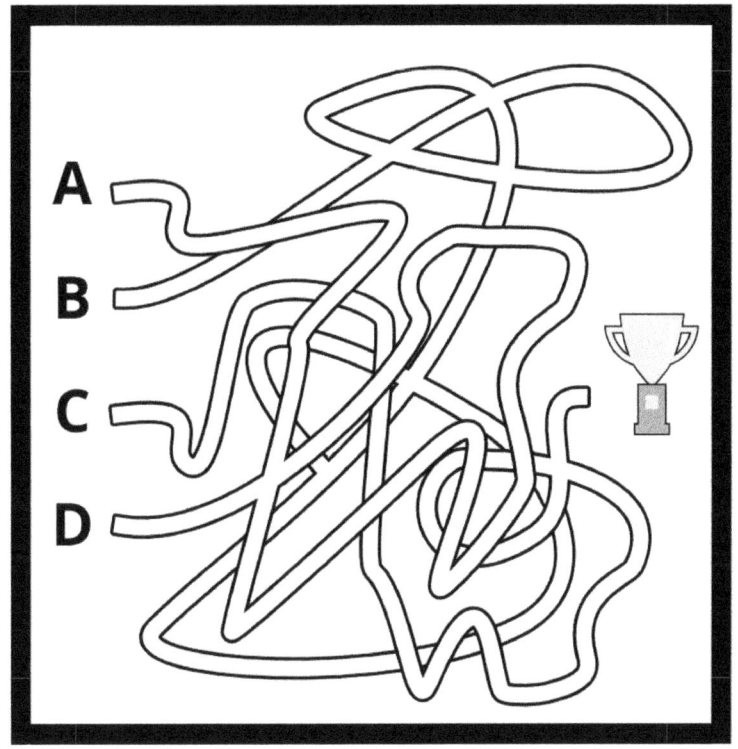

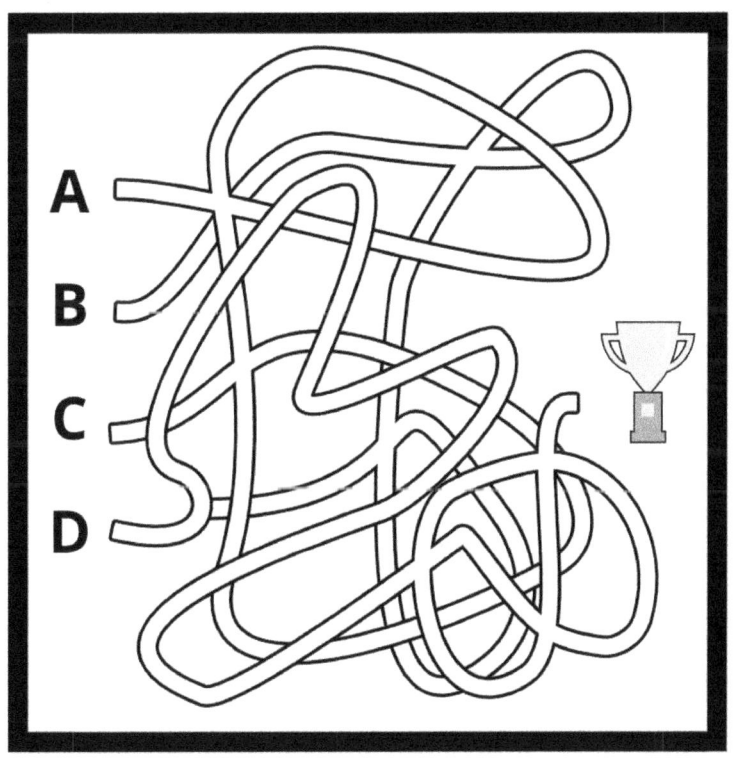

SOLUTION

FIND THE RIGHT WAY

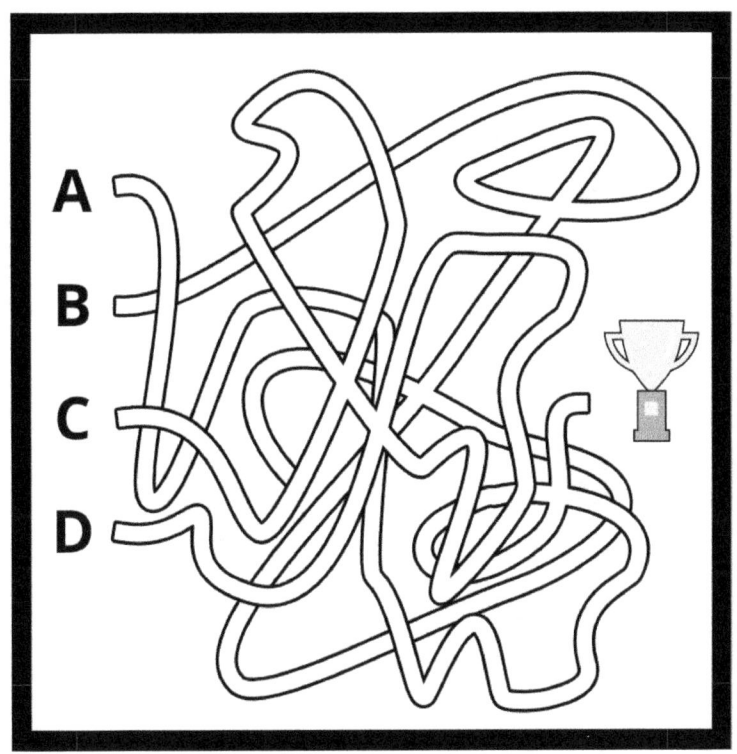

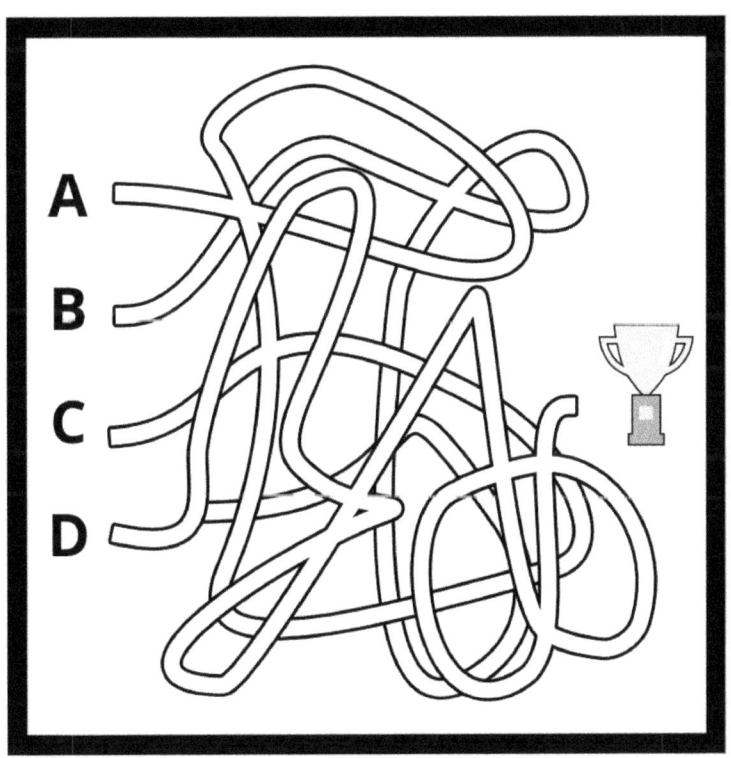

SOLUTION

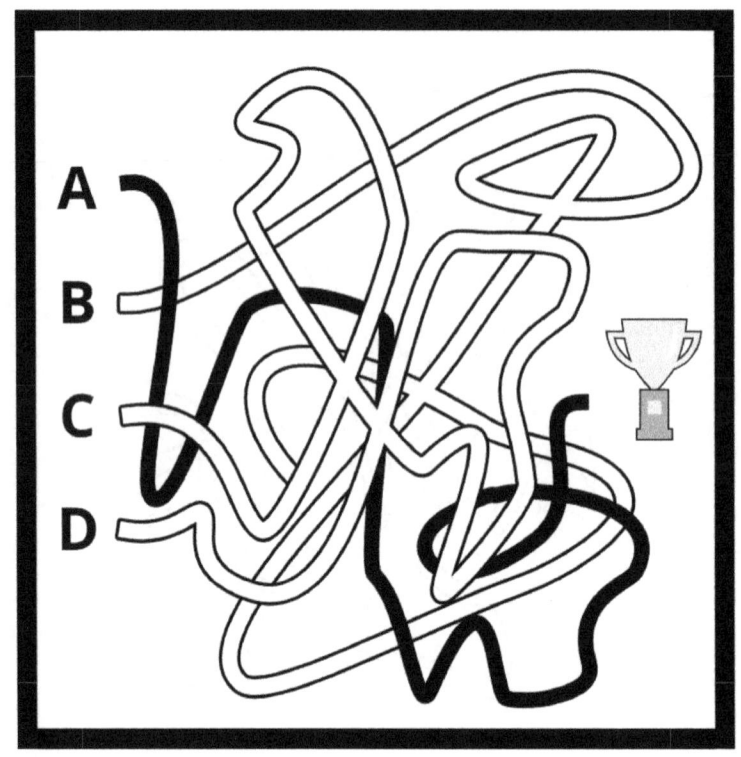

FIND THE RIGHT WAY

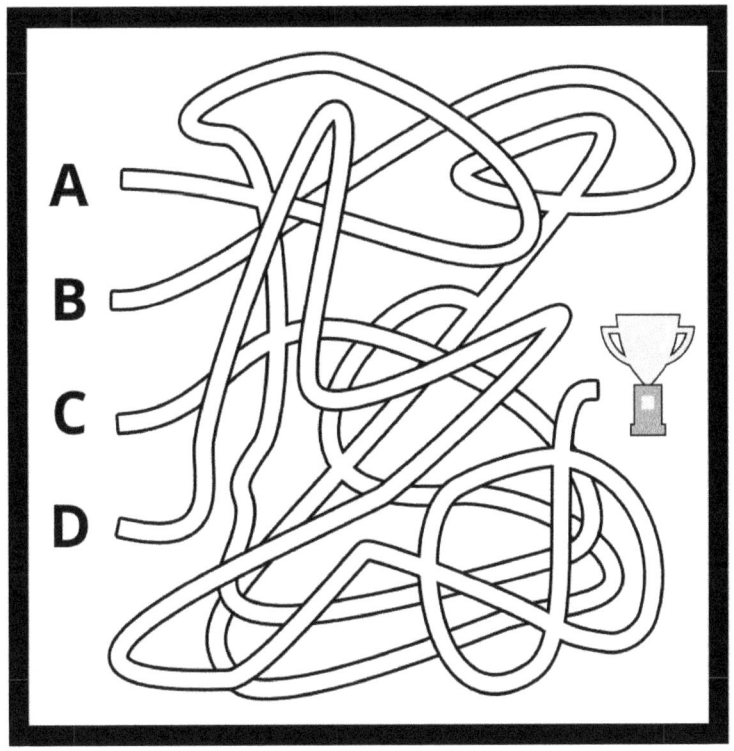

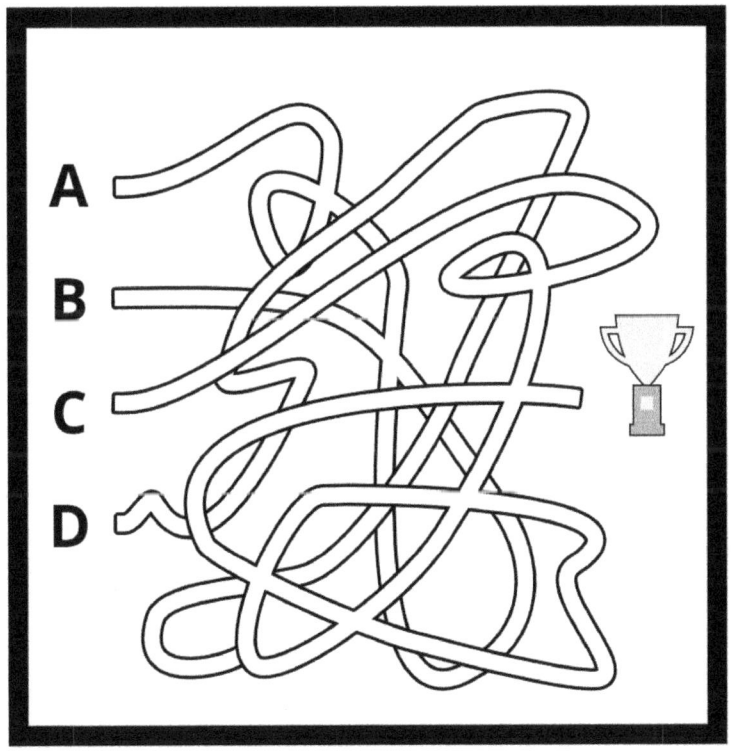

SOLUTION

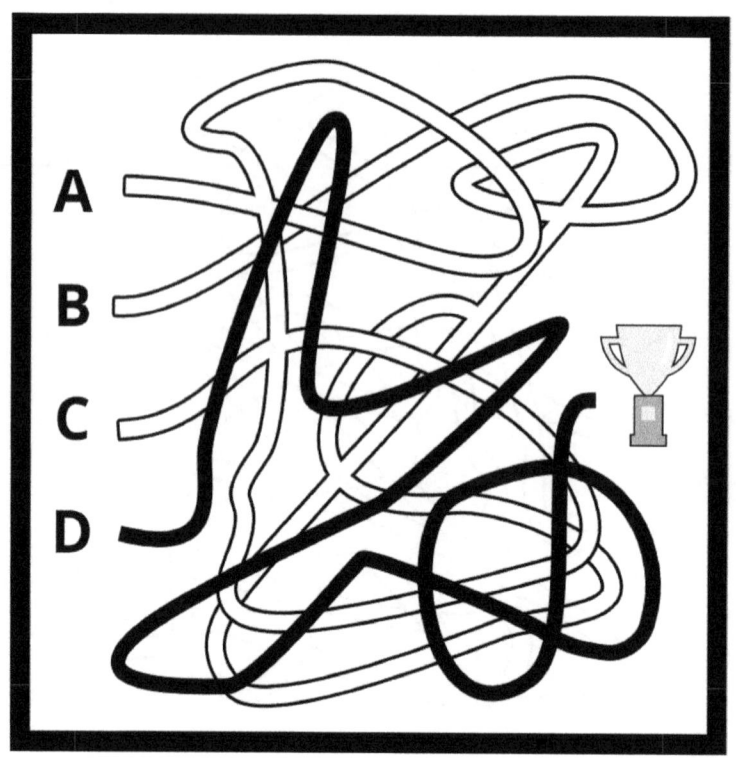

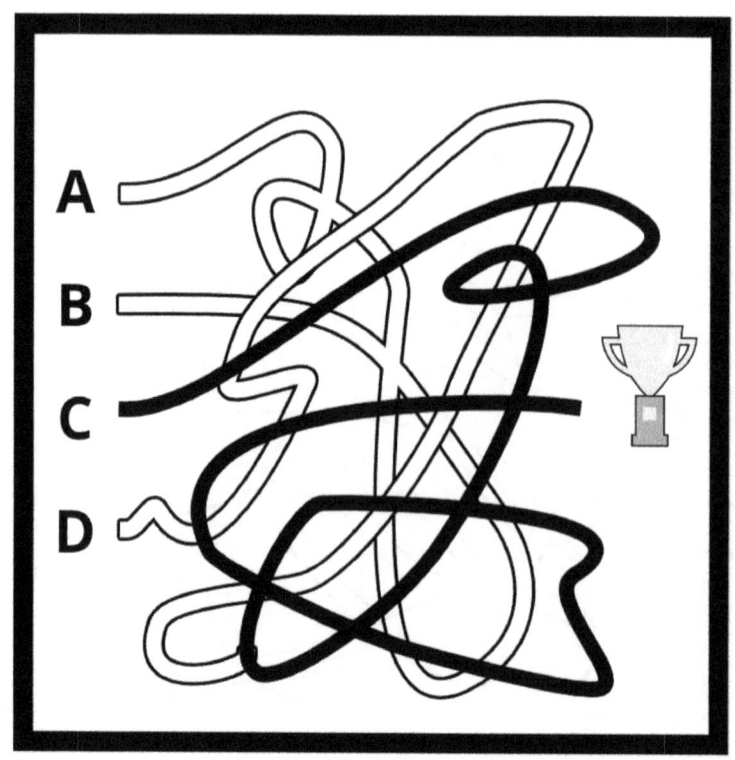

FIND THE RIGHT WAY

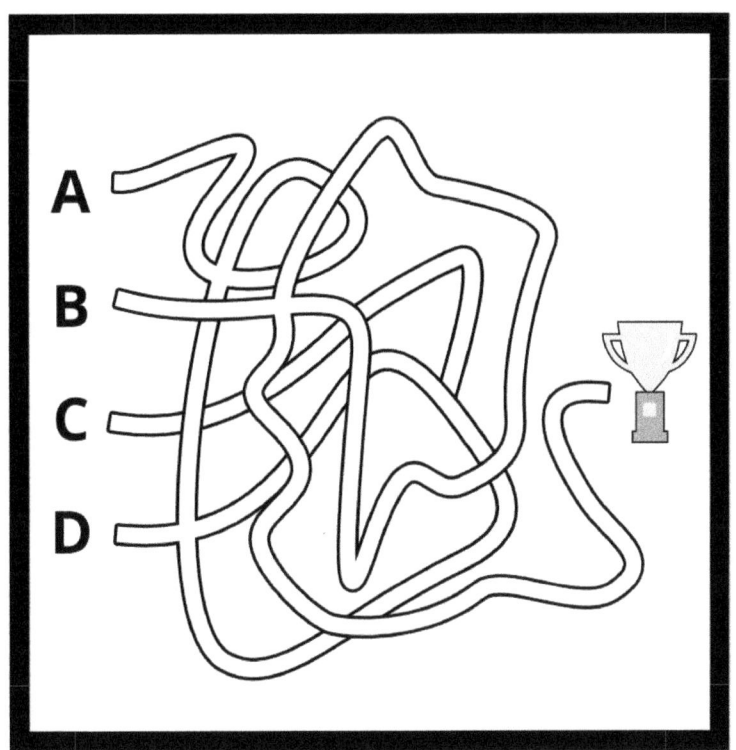

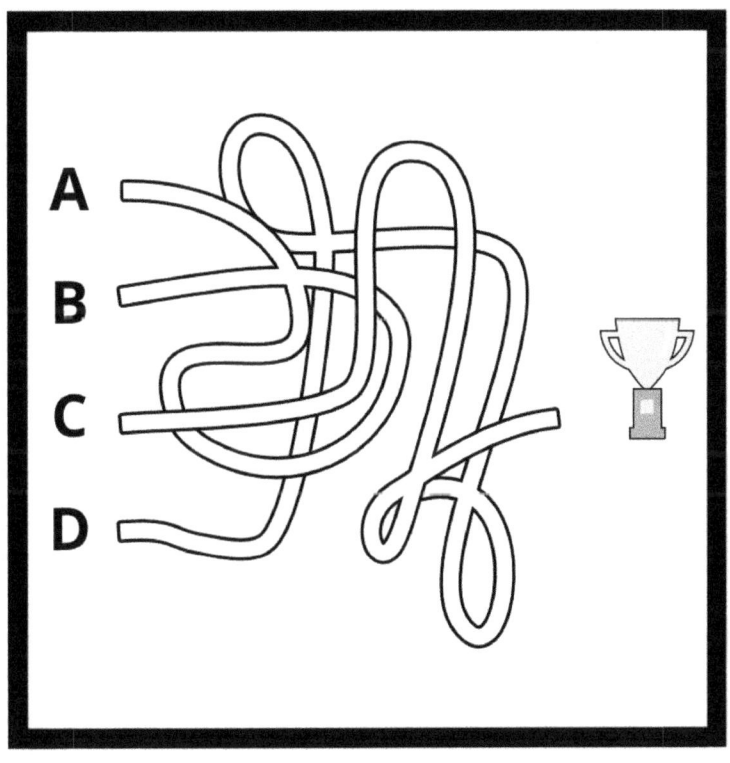

SOLUTION

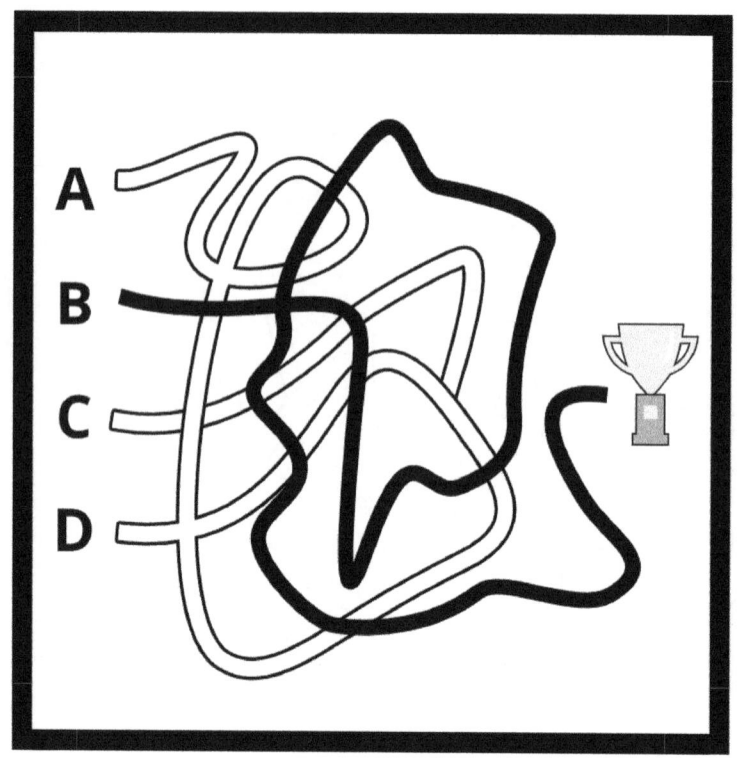

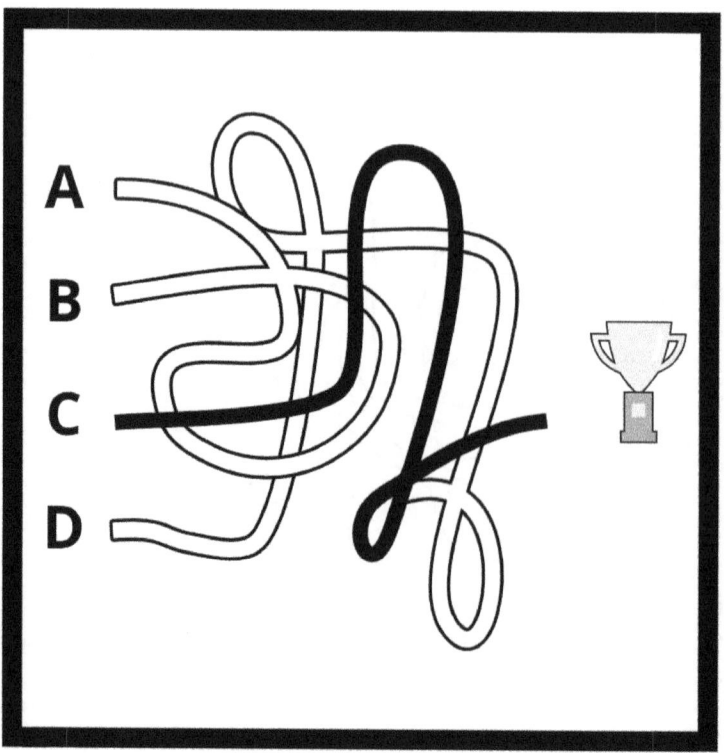

FIND THE RIGHT WAY

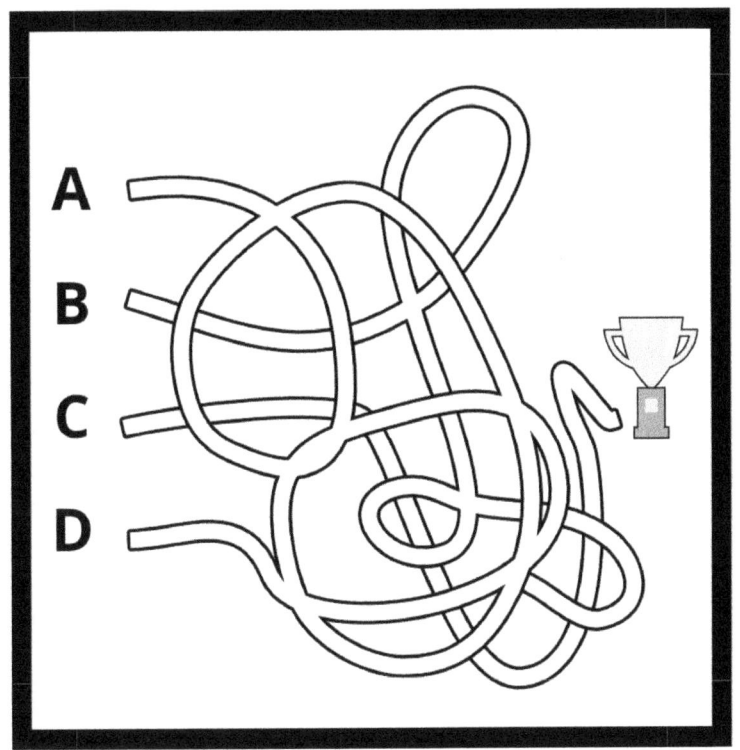

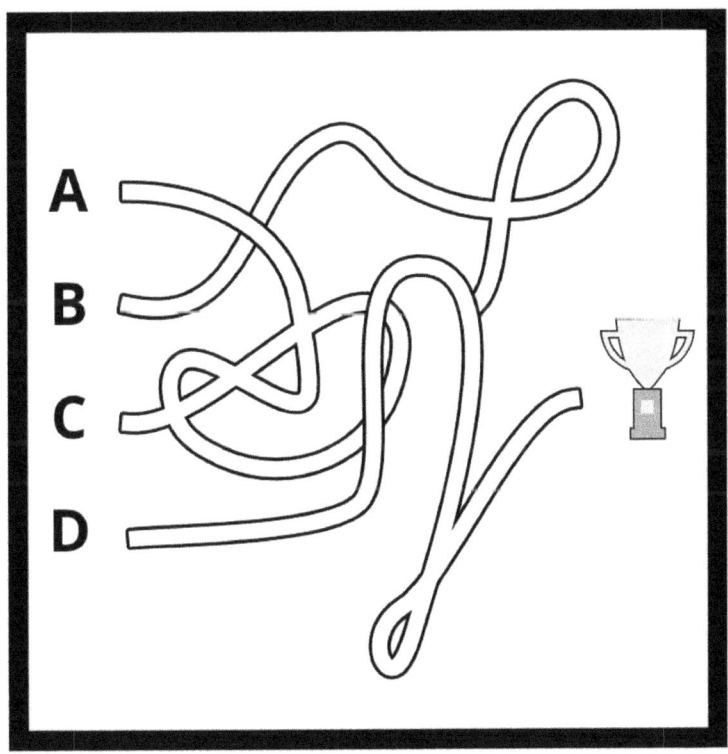

SOLUTION

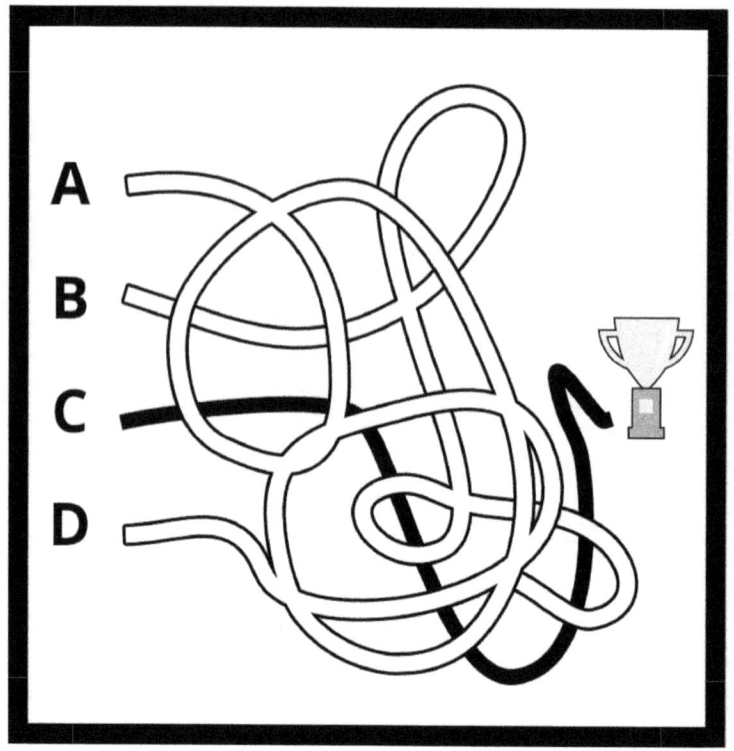

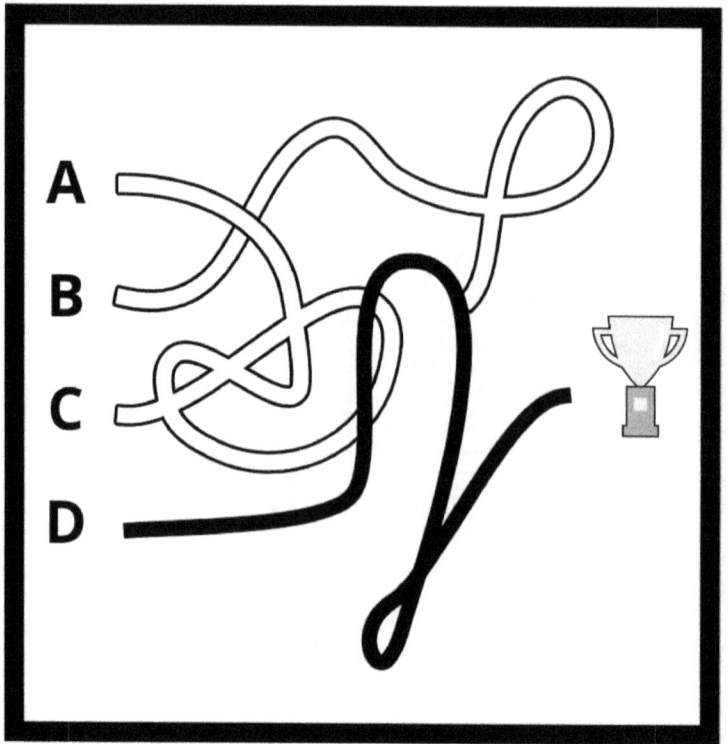

FIND THE RIGHT WAY

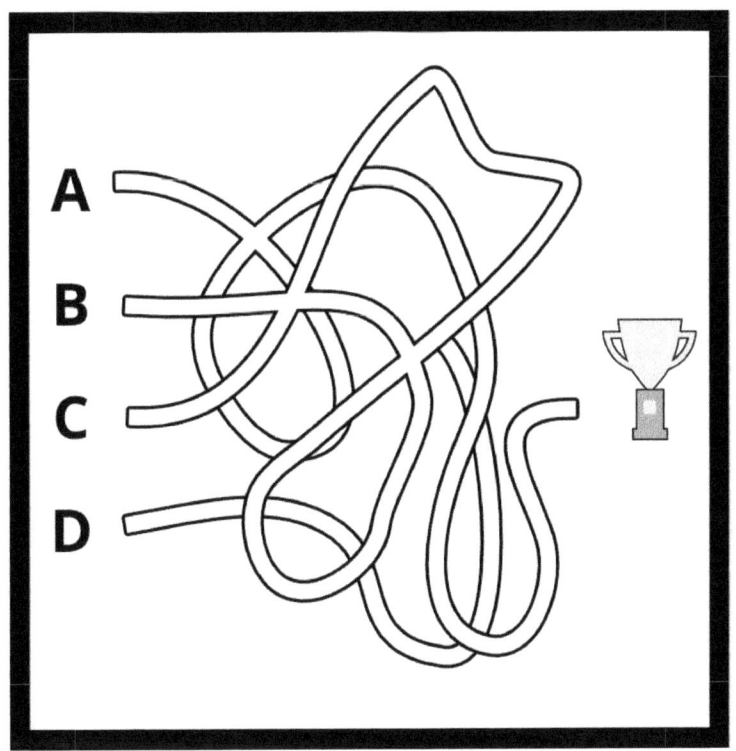

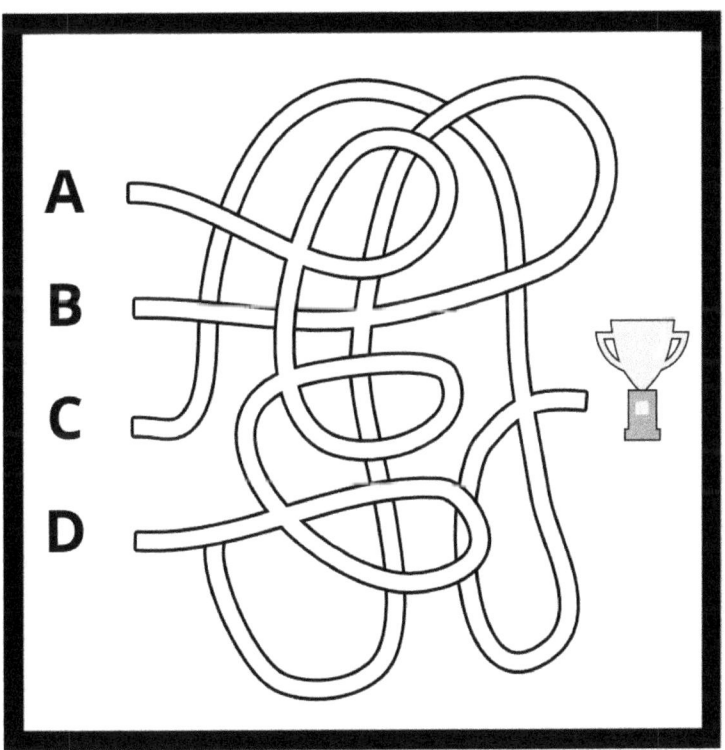

SOLUTION

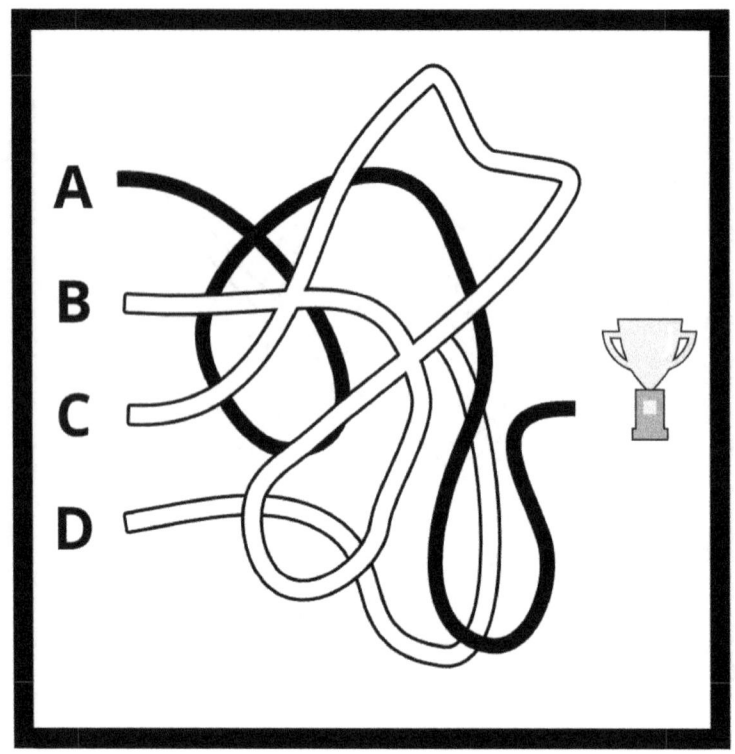

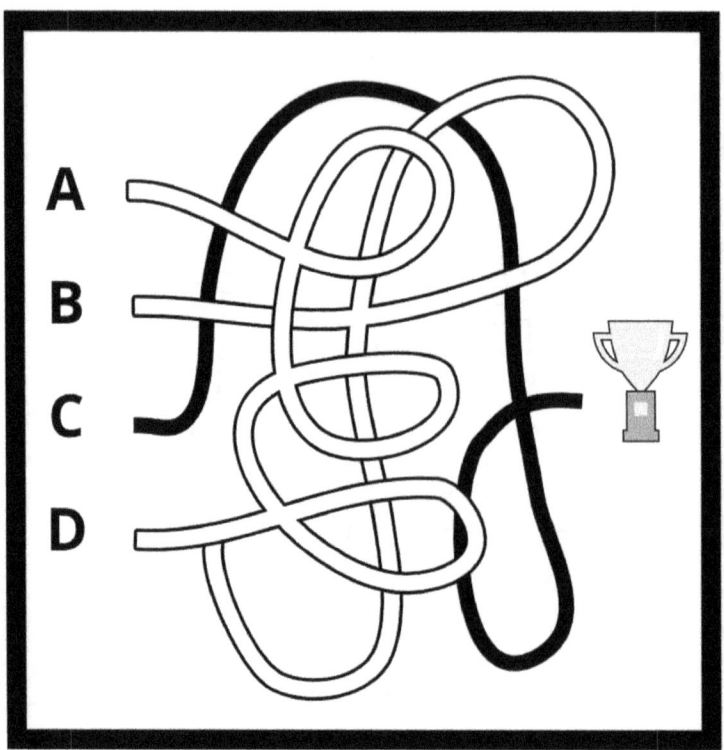

FIND THE RIGHT WAY

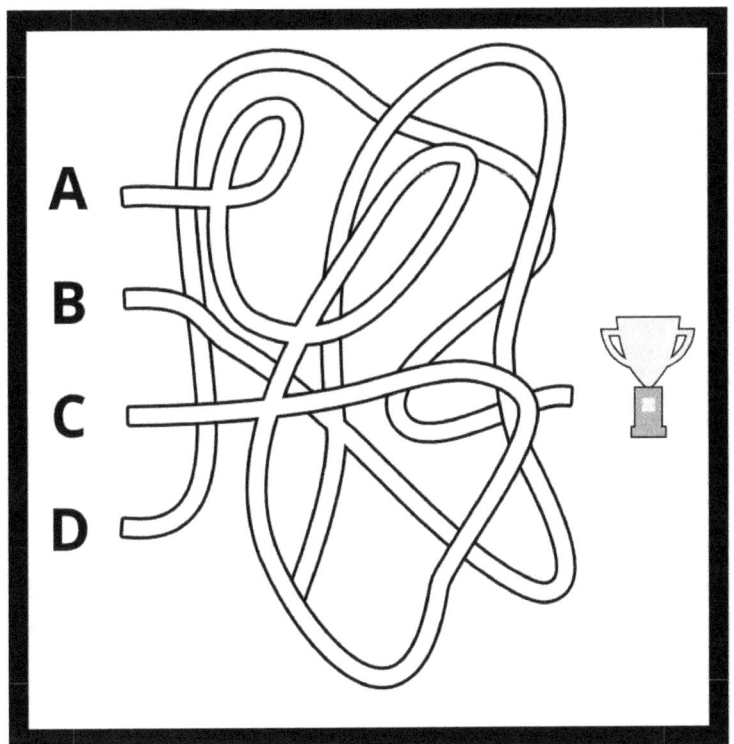

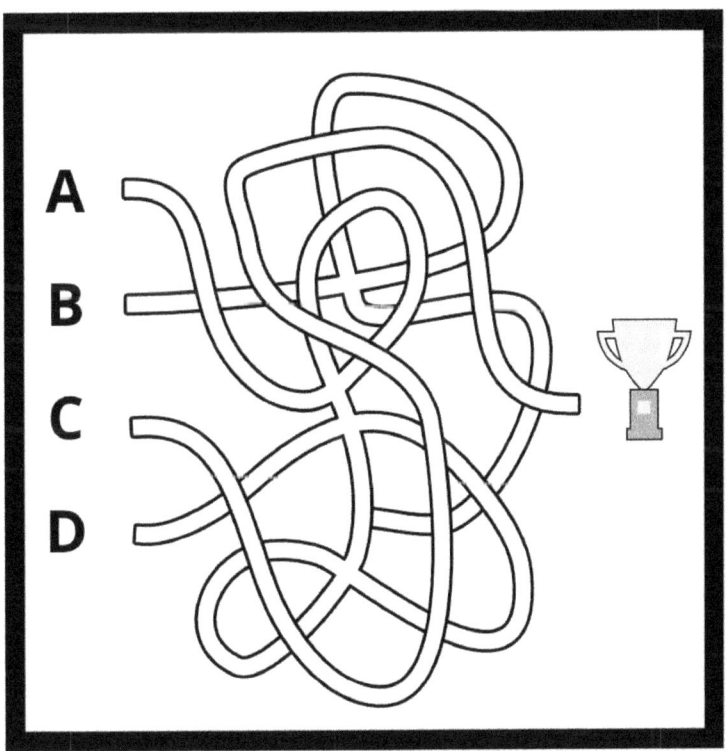

SOLUTION

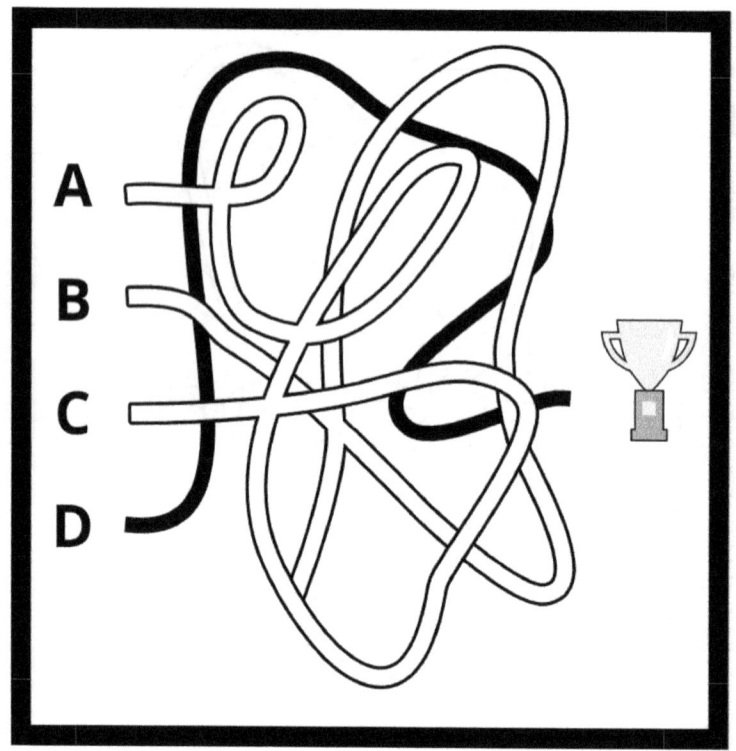

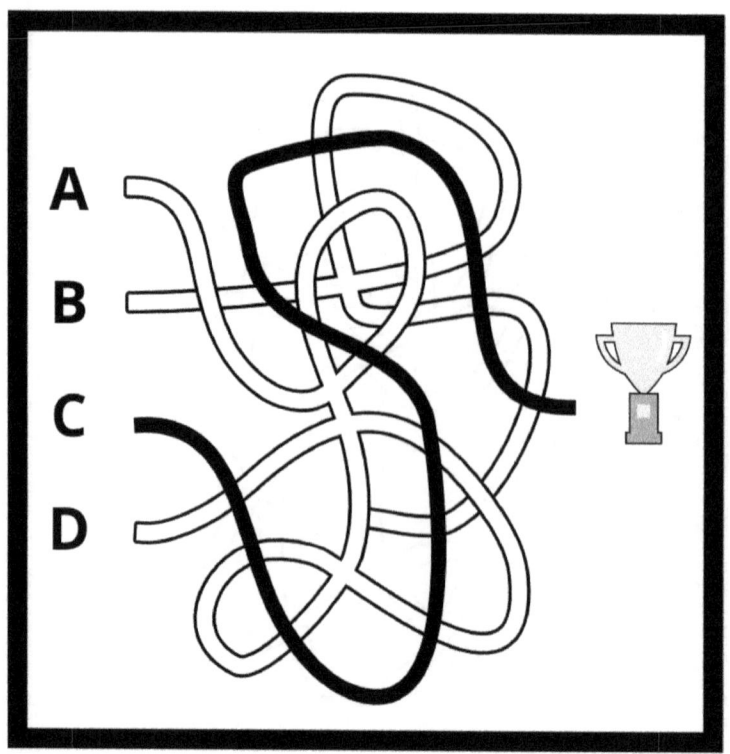

FIND THE RIGHT WAY

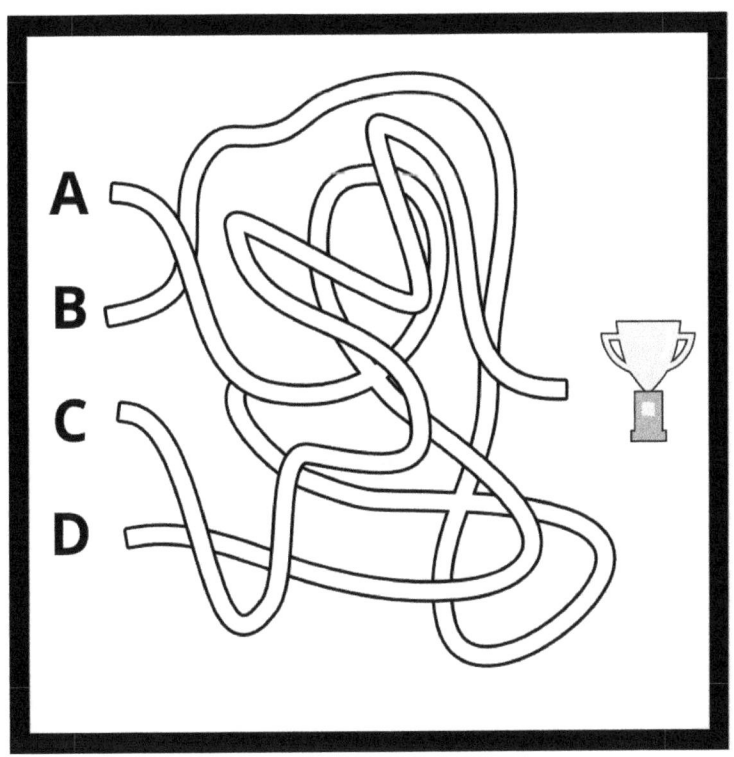

SOLUTION

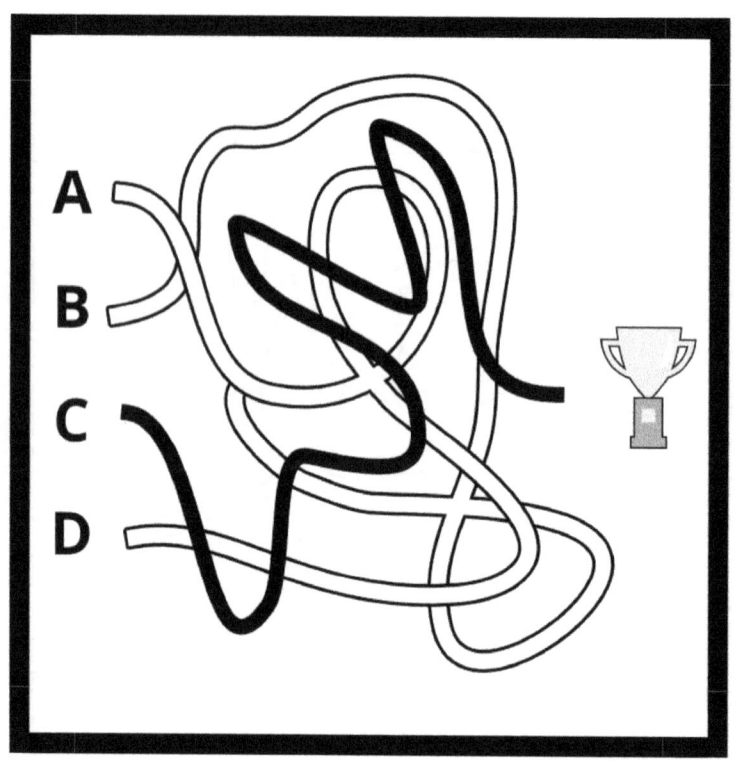

FIND THE SINGLE ONE

SOLUTION

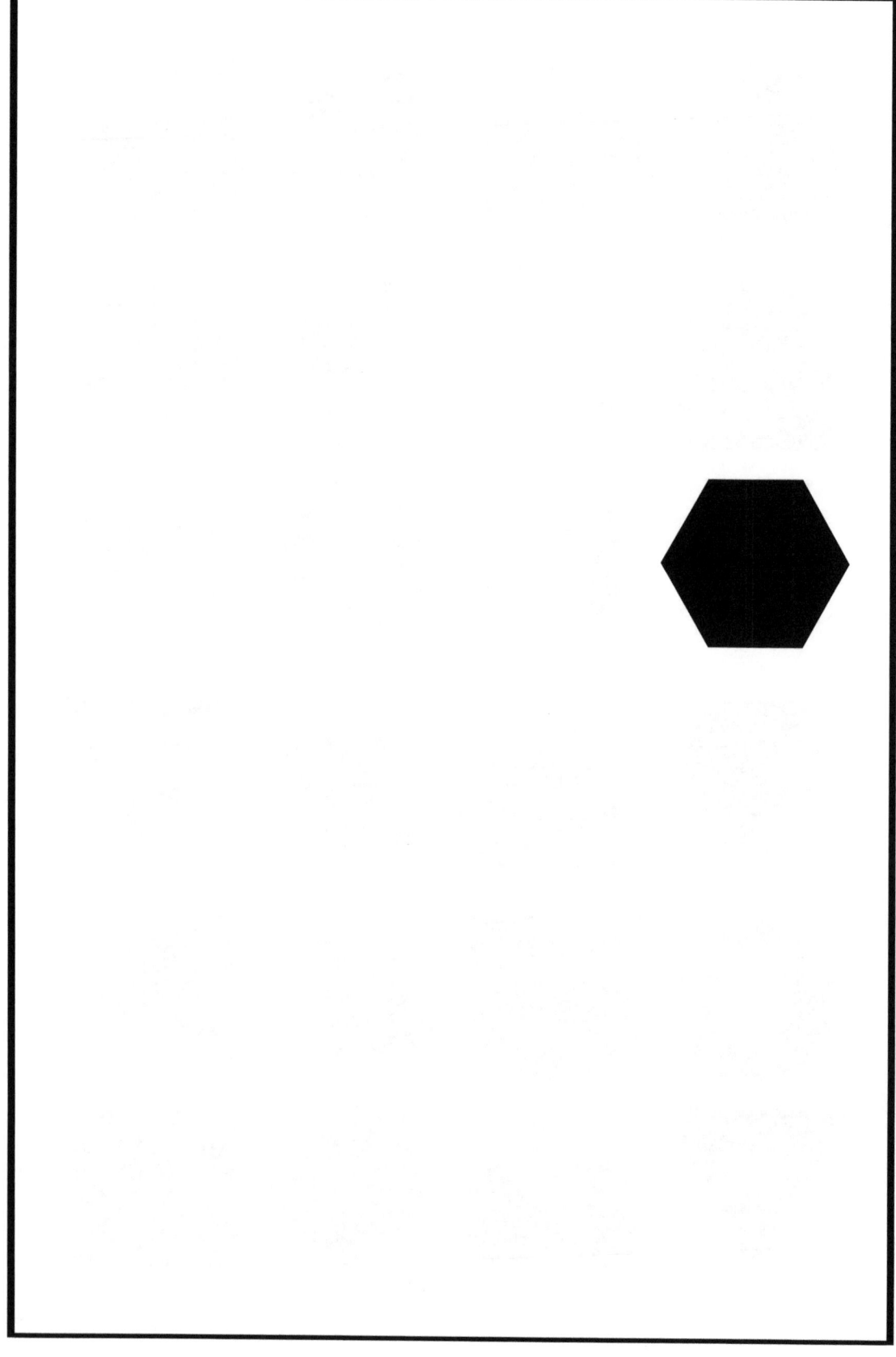

FIND THE SINGLE ONE

SOLUTION

FIND THE SINGLE ONE

SOLUTION

FIND THE SINGLE ONE

SOLUTION

FIND THE SINGLE ONE

SOLUTION

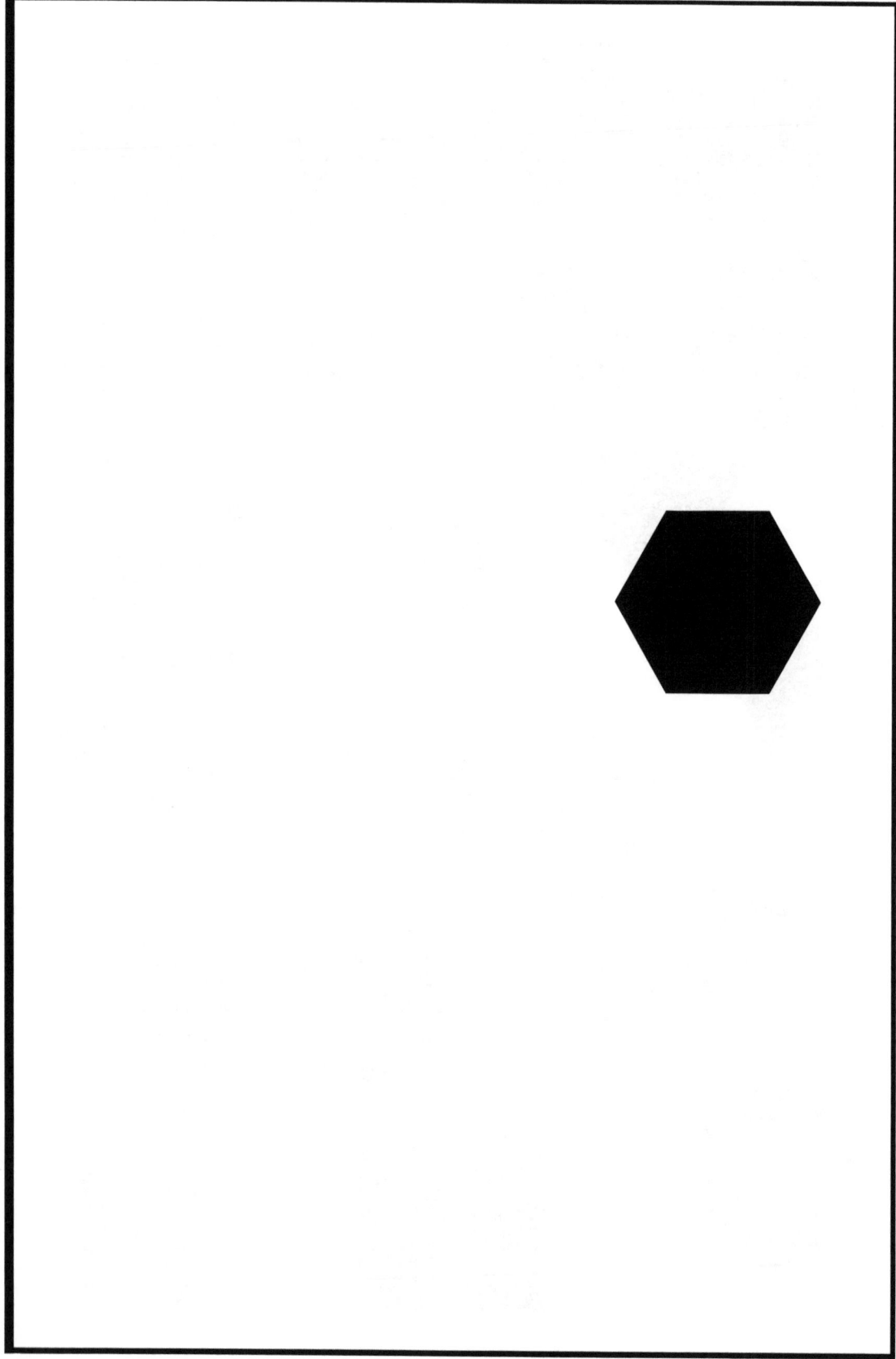

FIND THE SINGLE ONE

SOLUTION

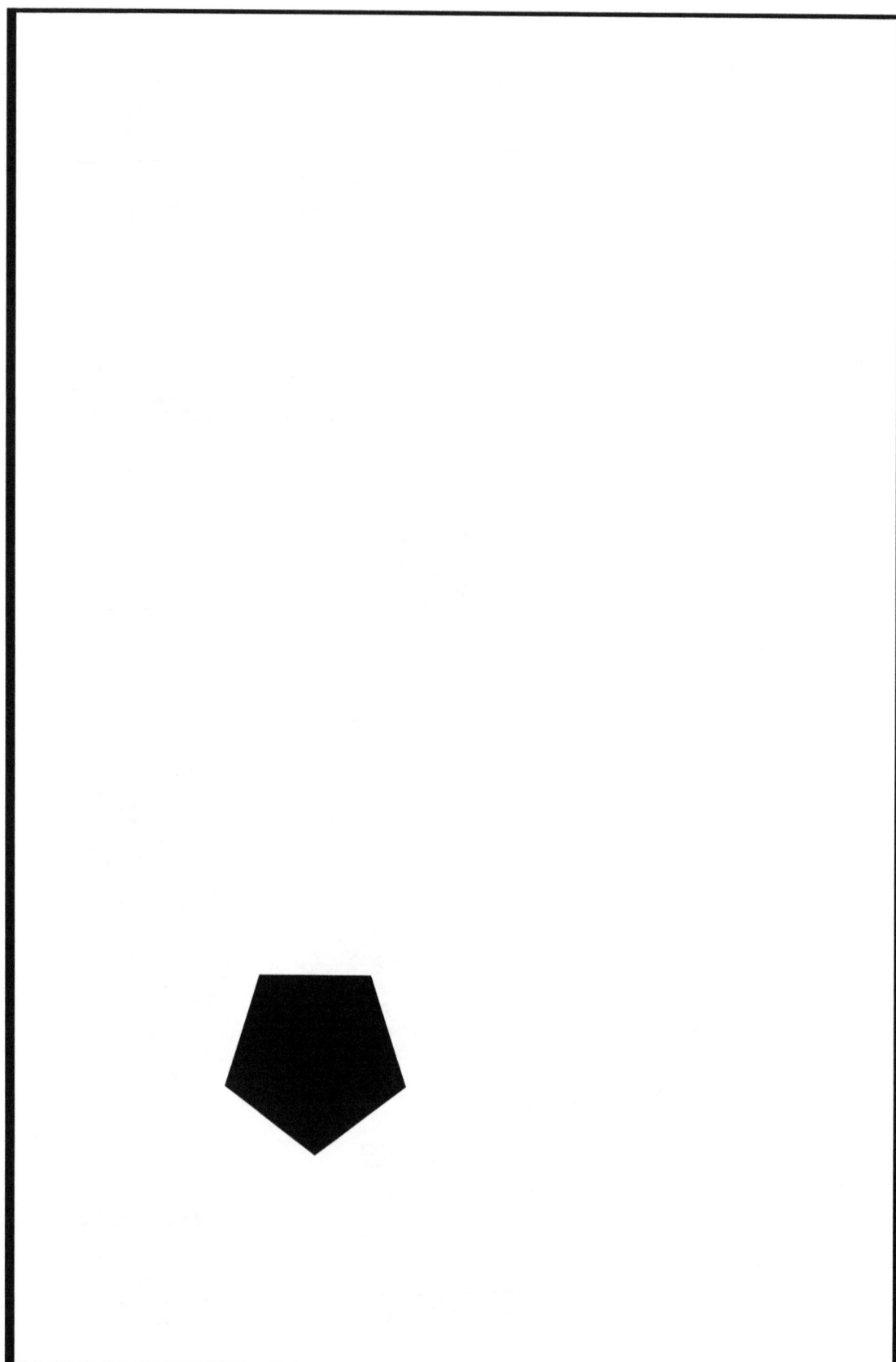

FIND THE SINGLE ONE

SOLUTION

FIND THE SINGLE ONE

SOLUTION

FIND THE SINGLE ONE

SOLUTION

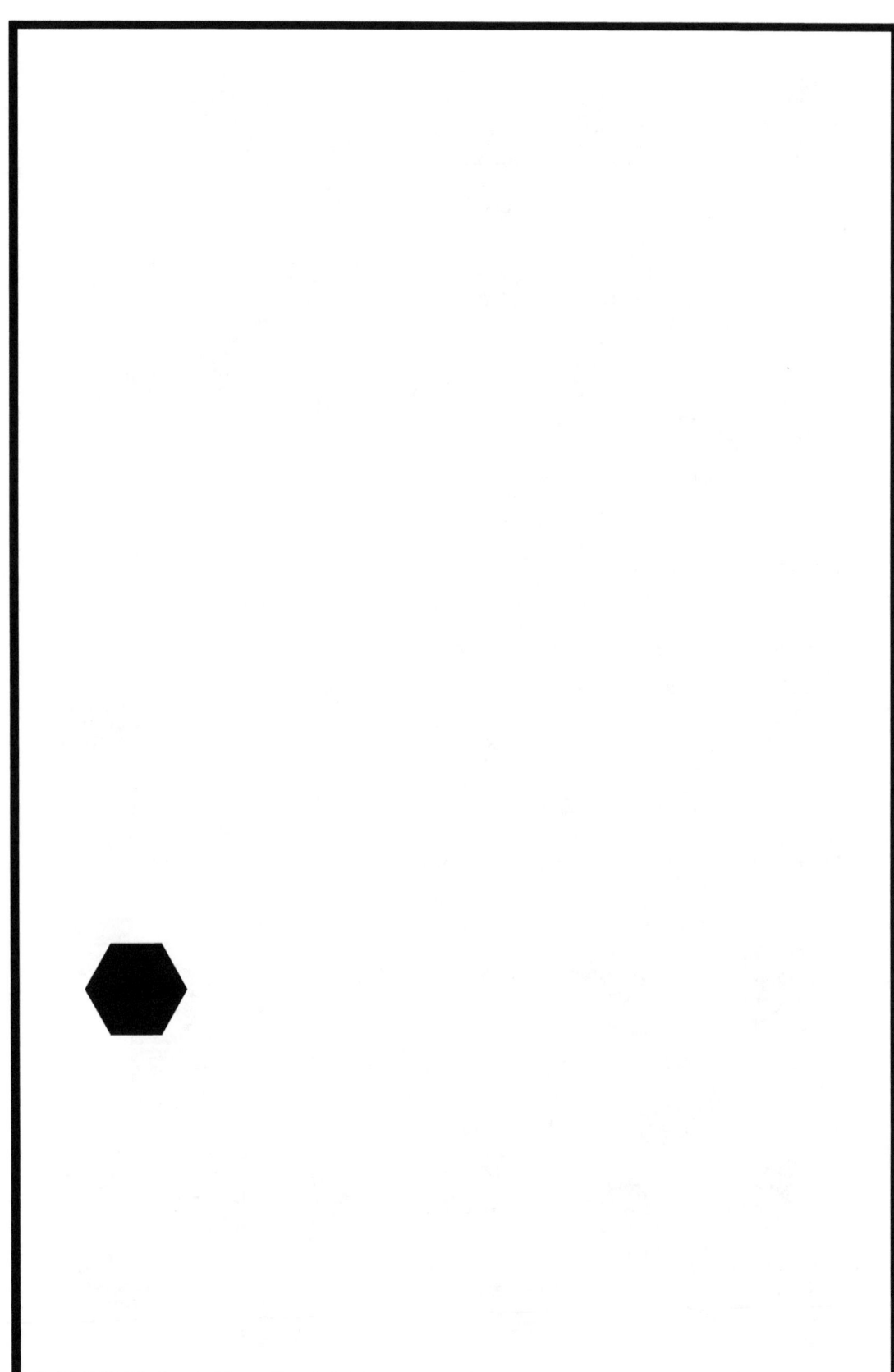

FIND THE SINGLE ONE

SOLUTION

FIND THE SINGLE ONE

SOLUTION

FIND THE SINGLE ONE

SOLUTION

FIND THE SINGLE ONE

SOLUTION

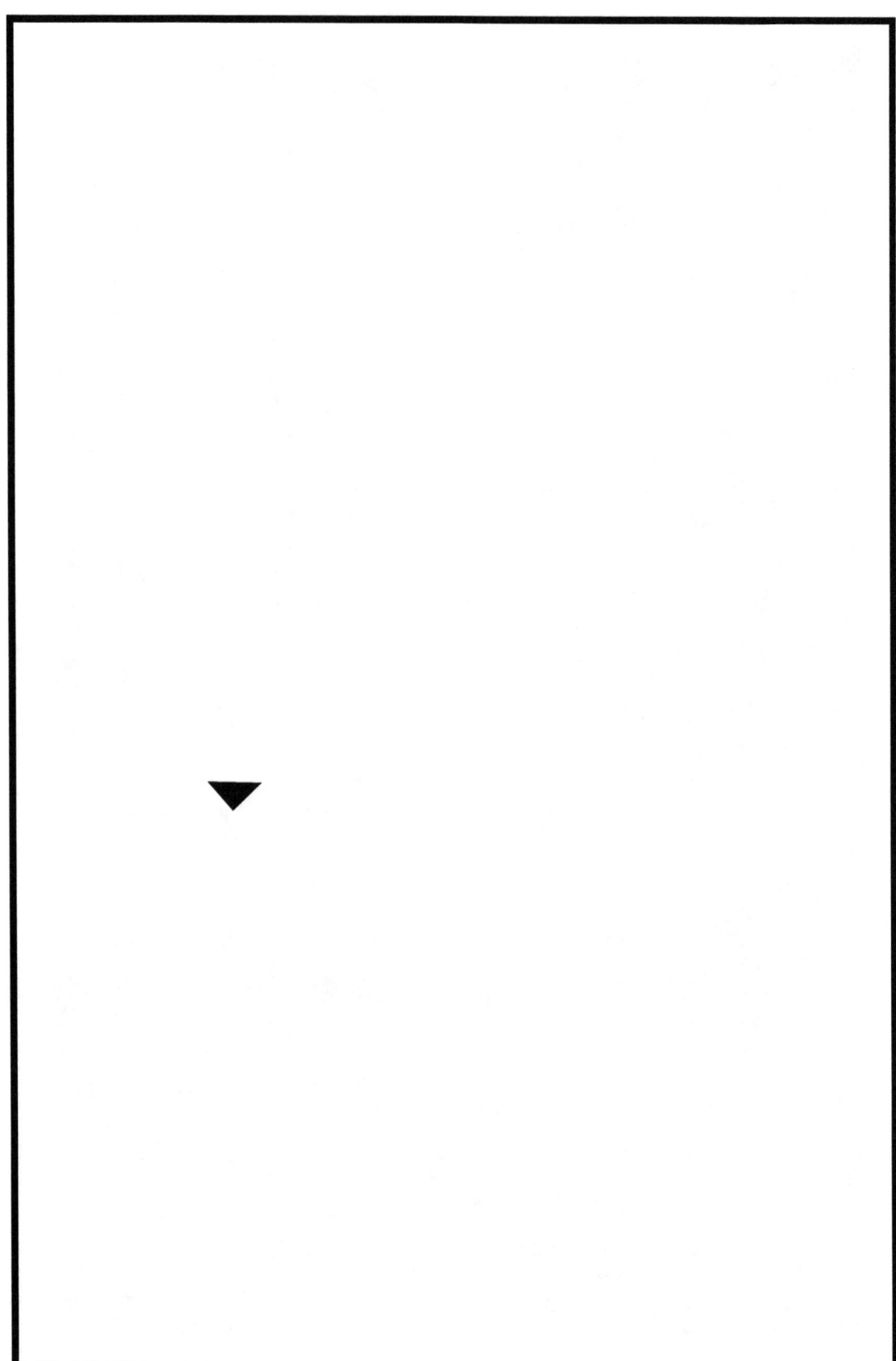

FIND THE SINGLE ONE

SOLUTION

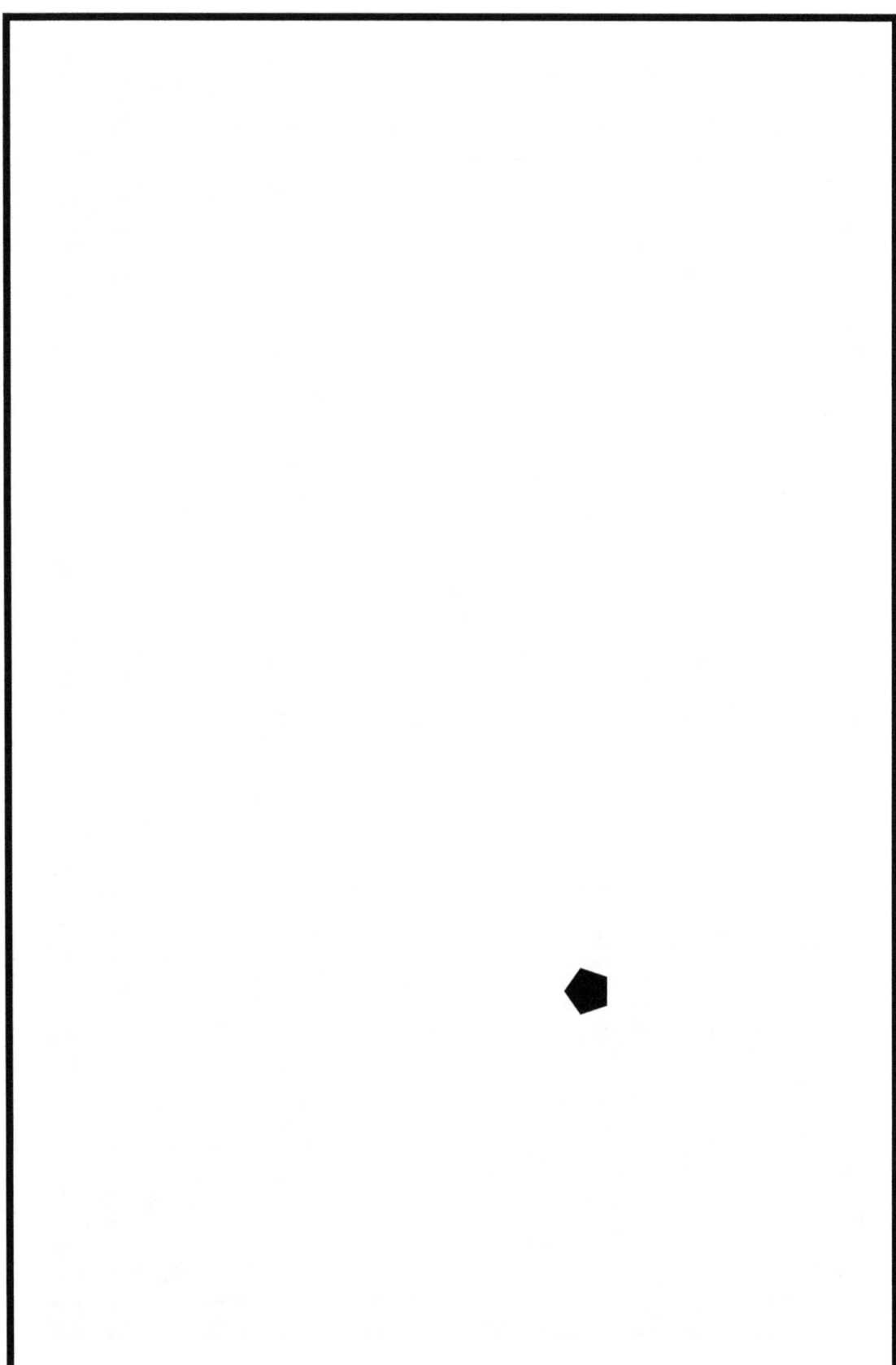

FOUR IN A ROW

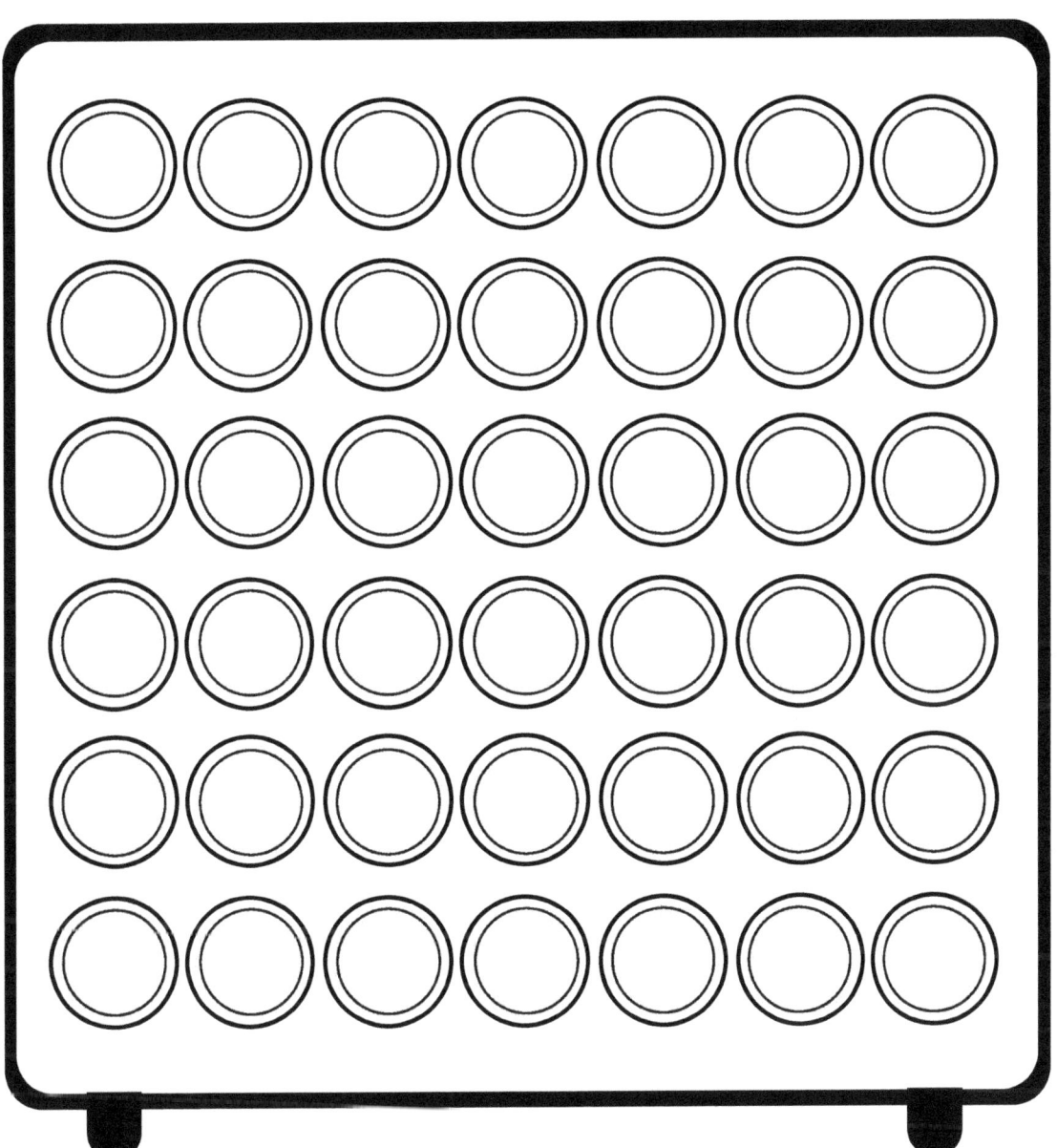

FOUR IN A ROW

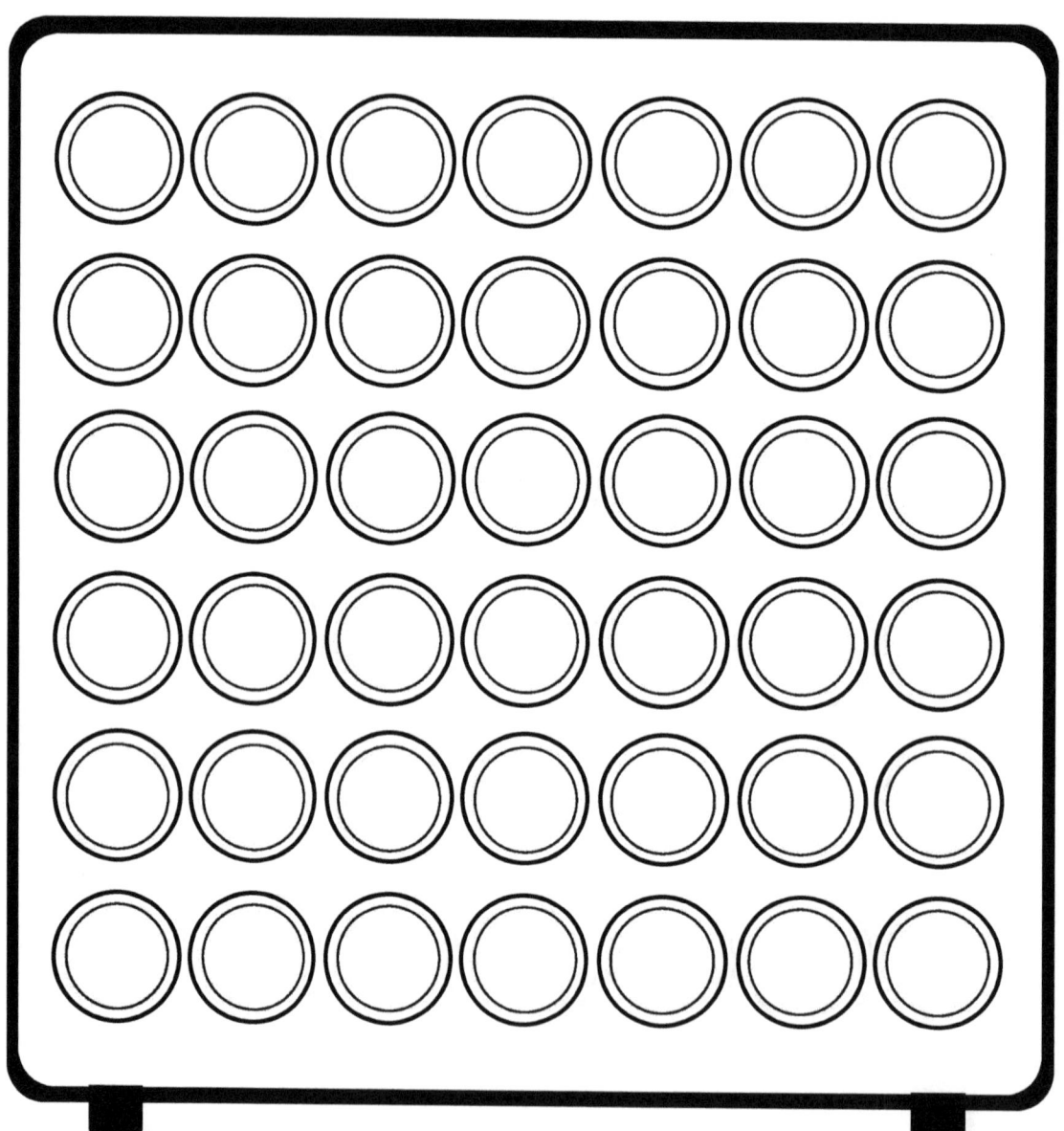

FOUR IN A ROW

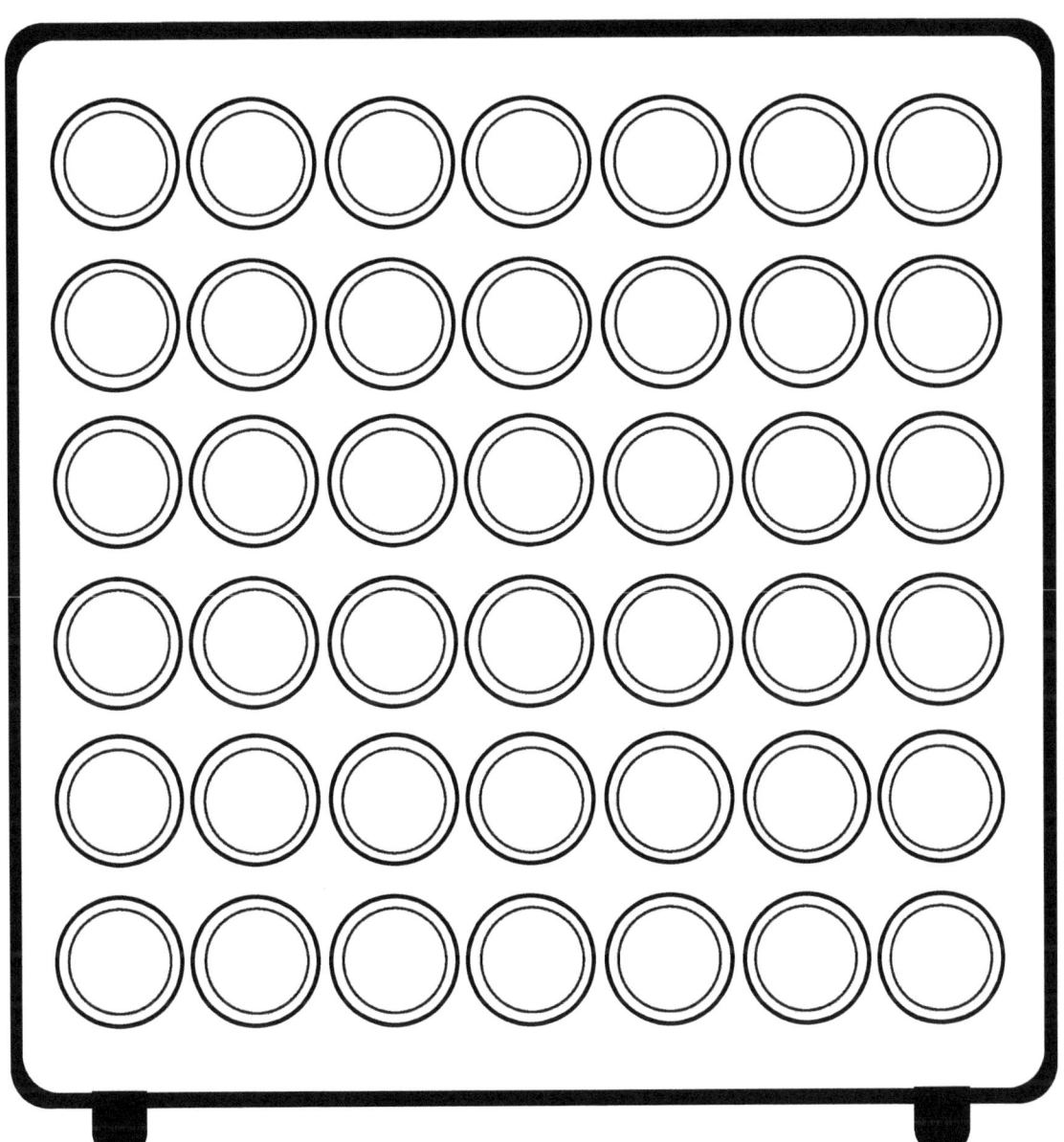

FOUR IN A ROW

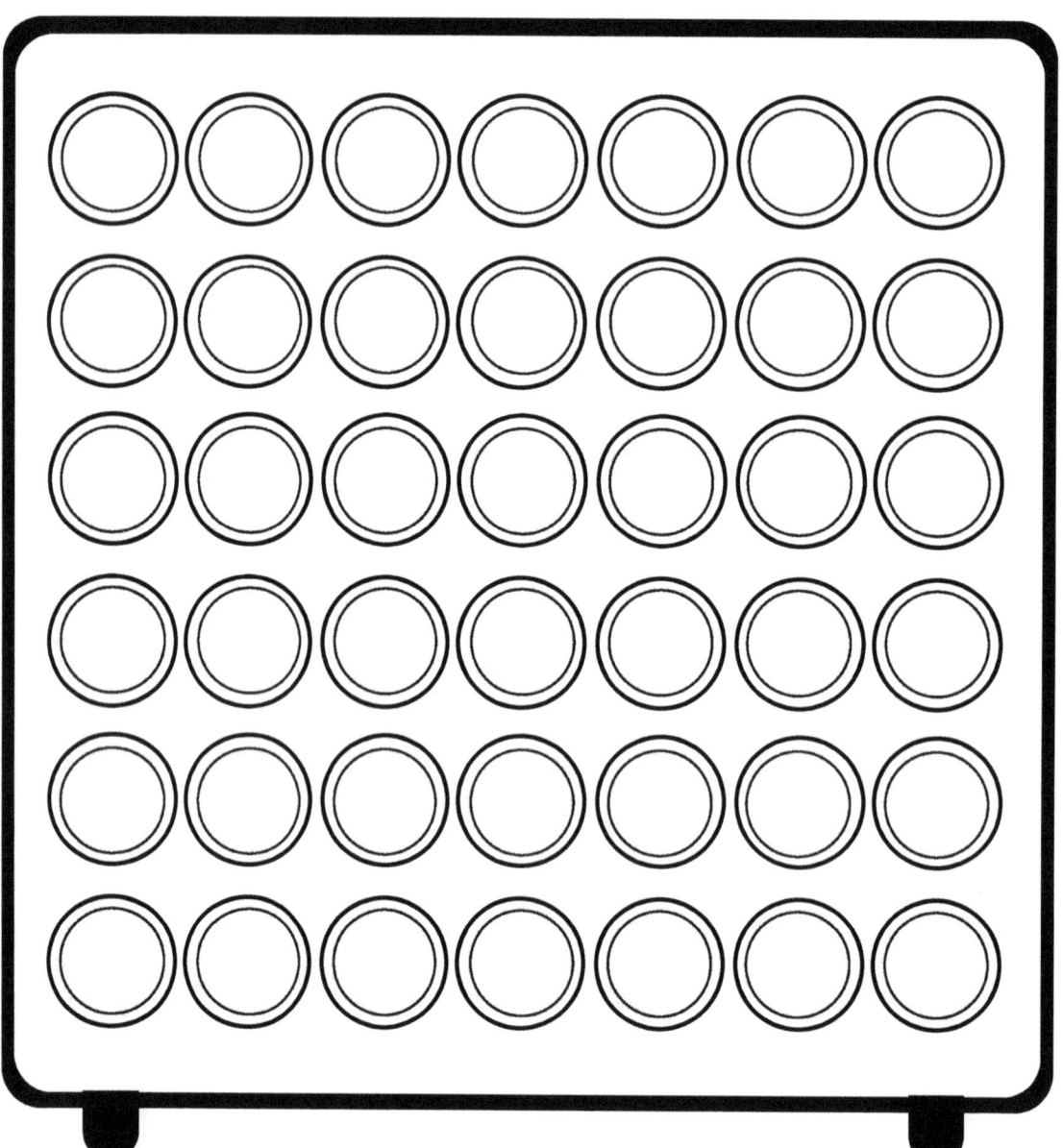

FOUR IN A ROW

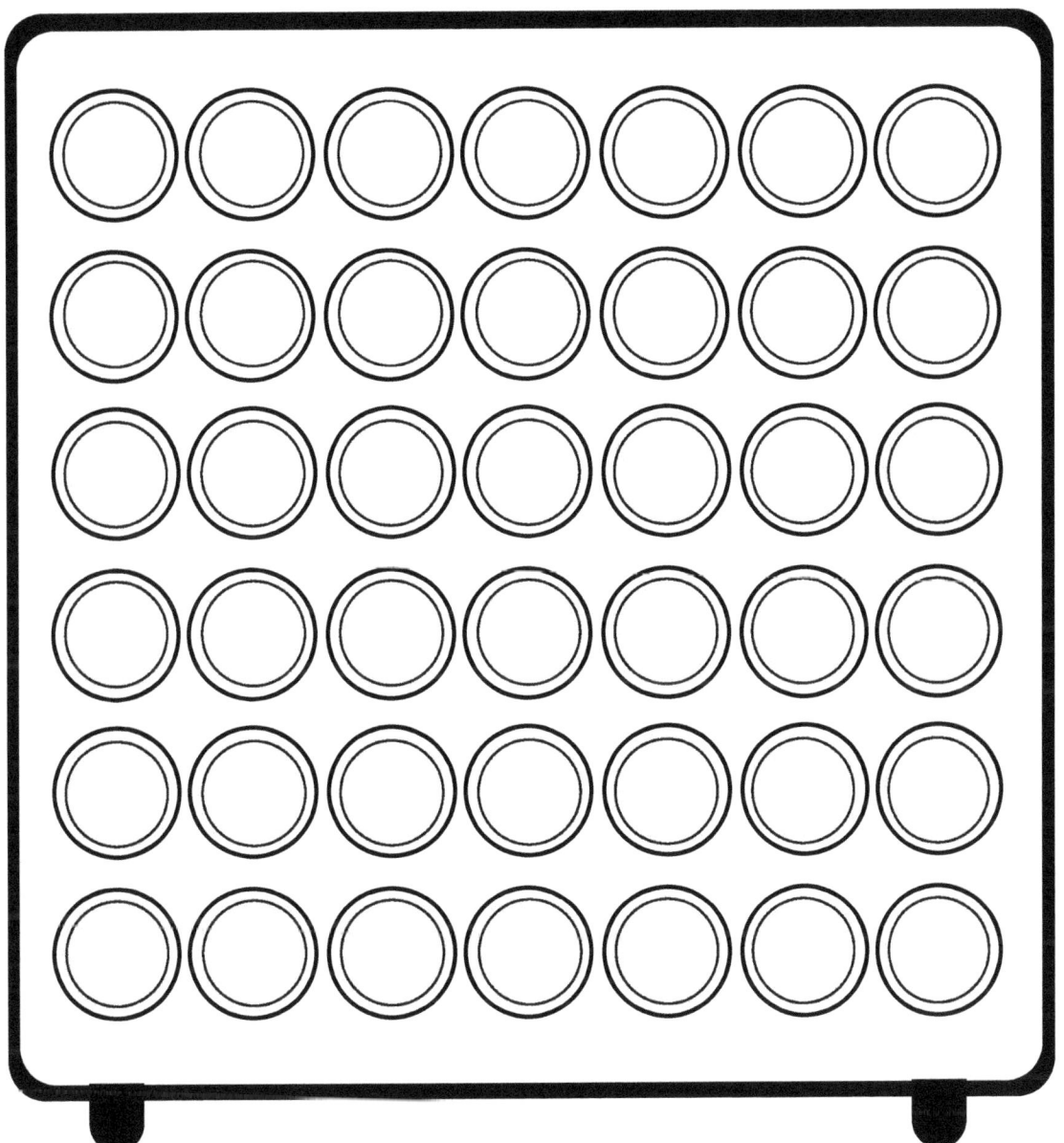

FOUR IN A ROW

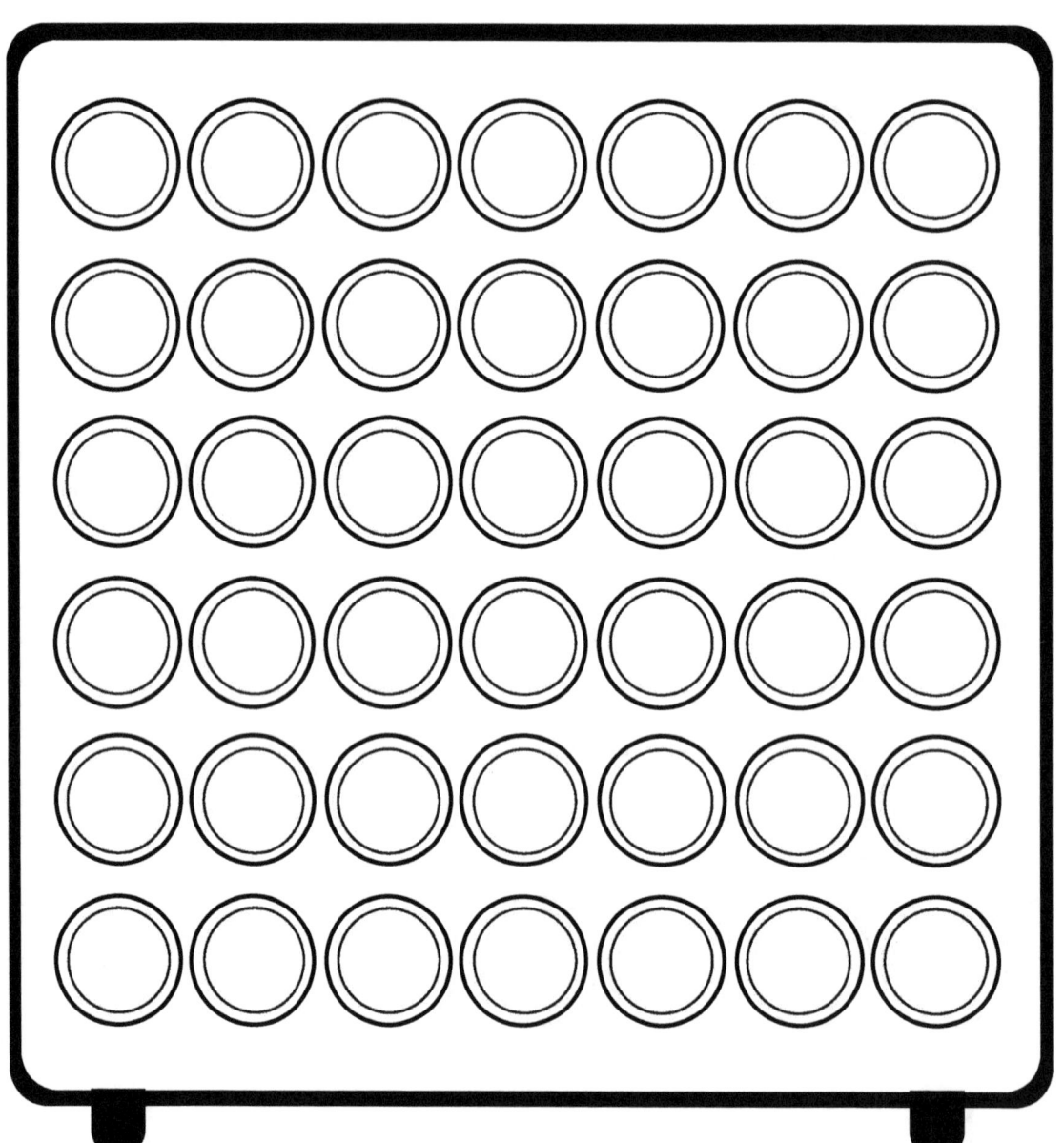

FOUR IN A ROW

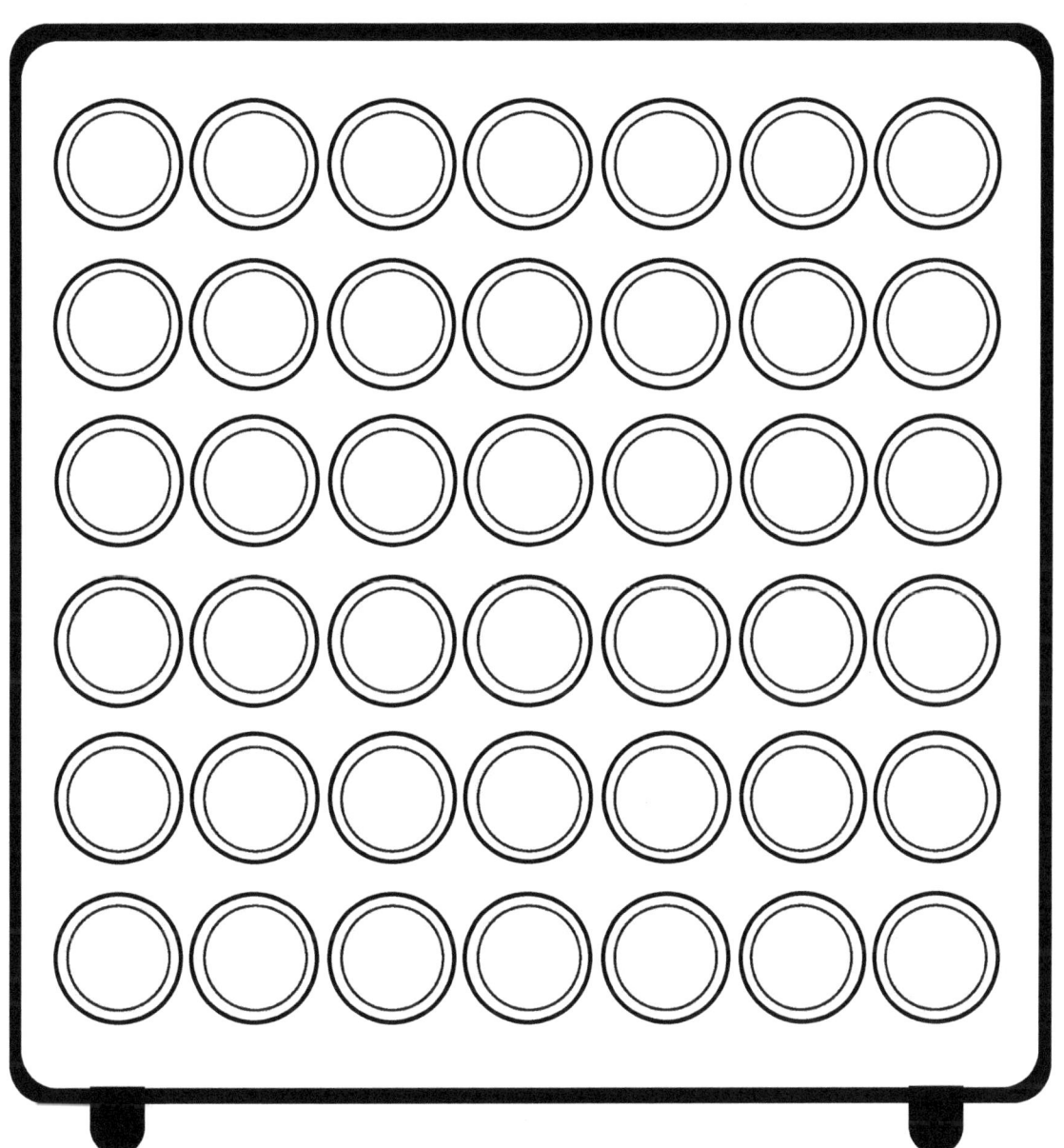

FOUR IN A ROW

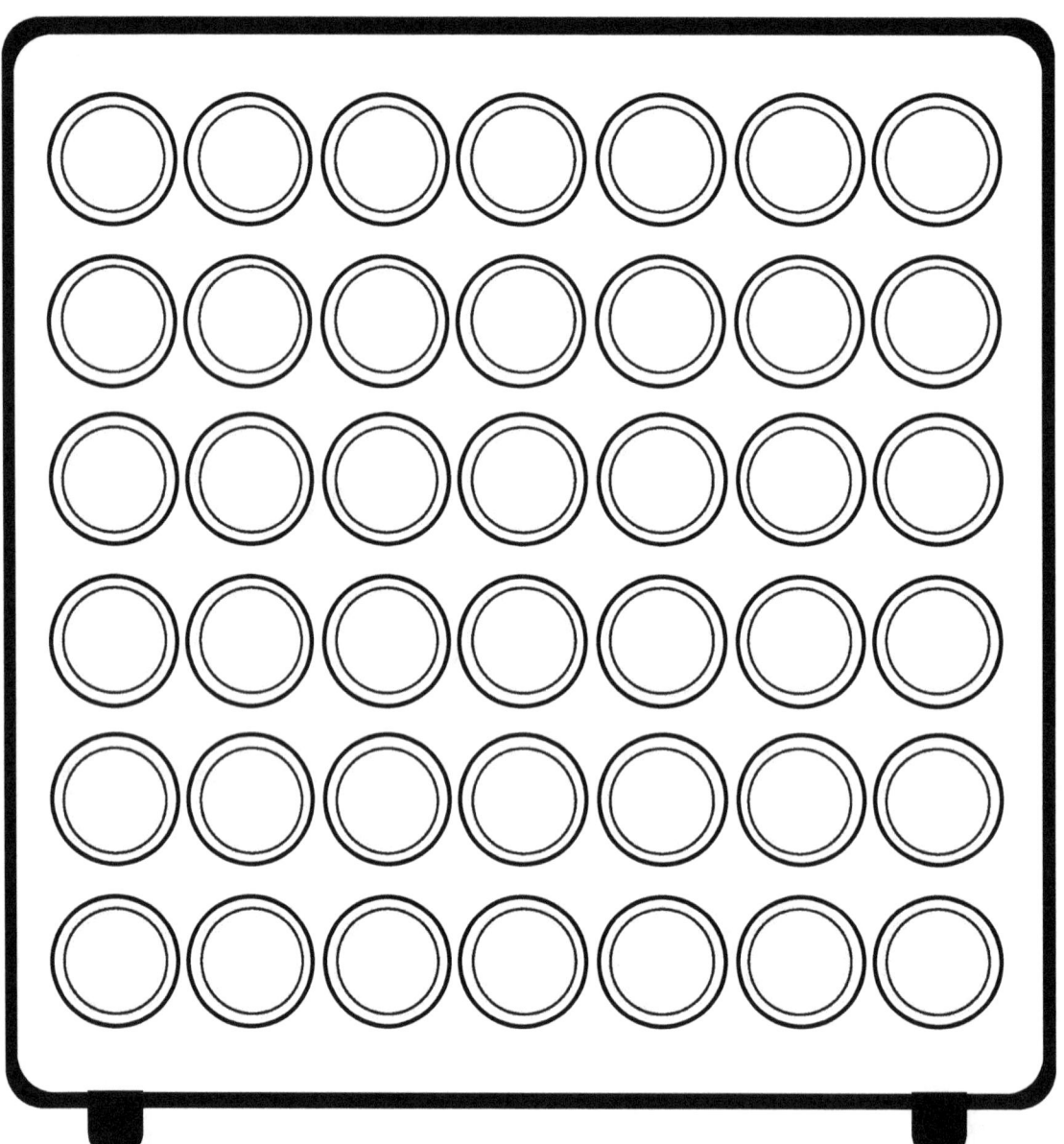

FOUR IN A ROW

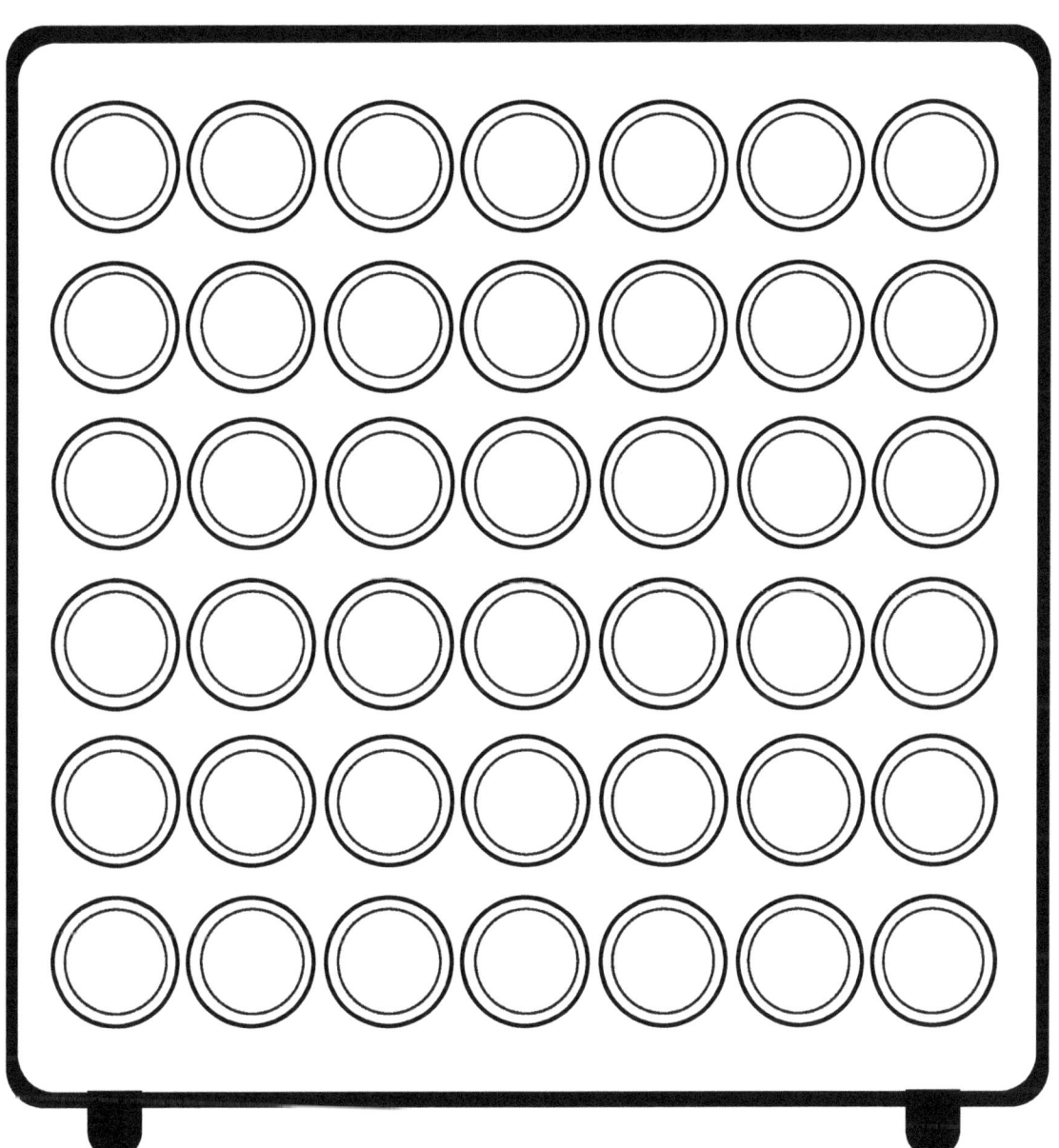

FOUR IN A ROW

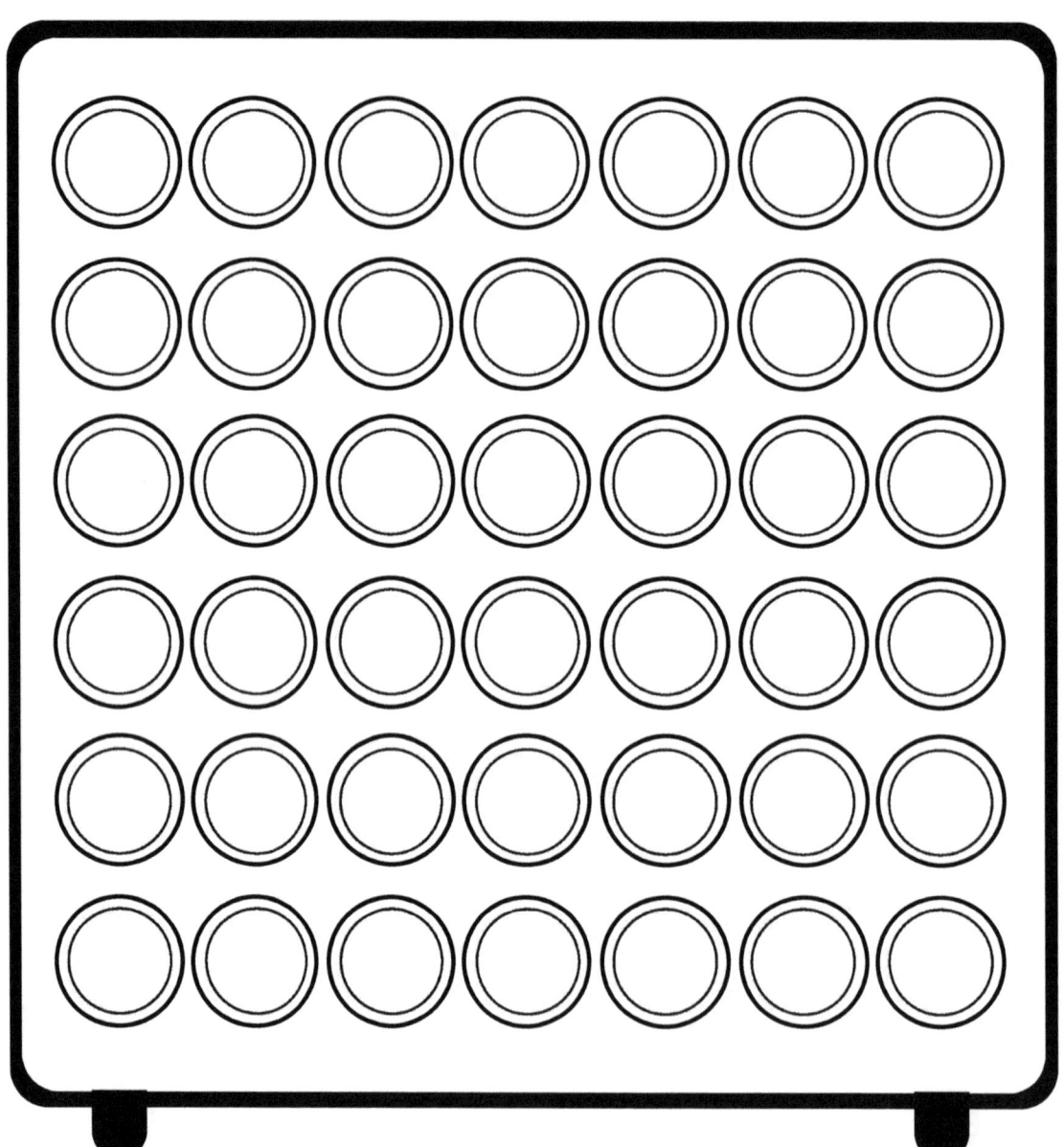

FOUR IN A ROW

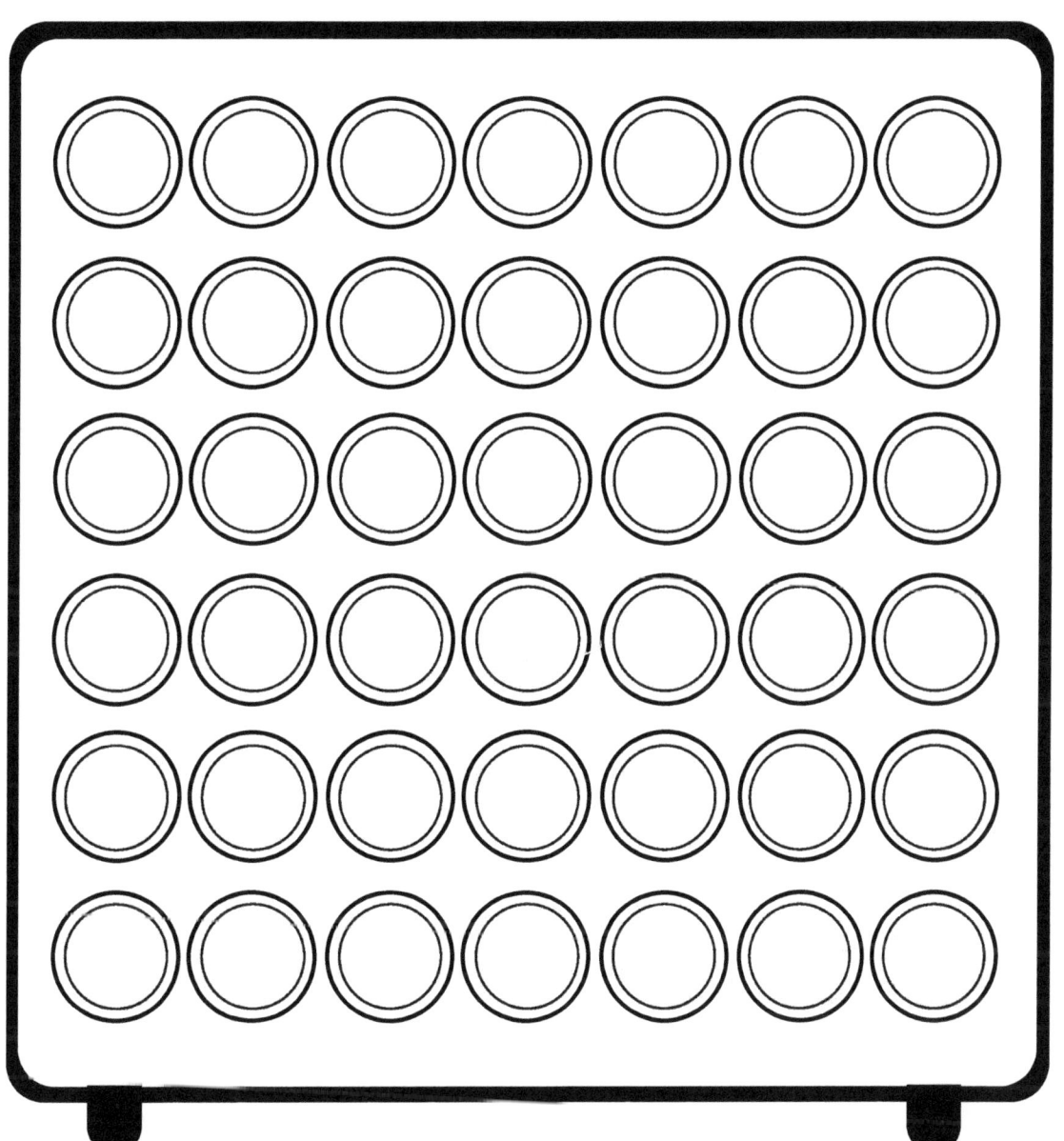

FOUR IN A ROW

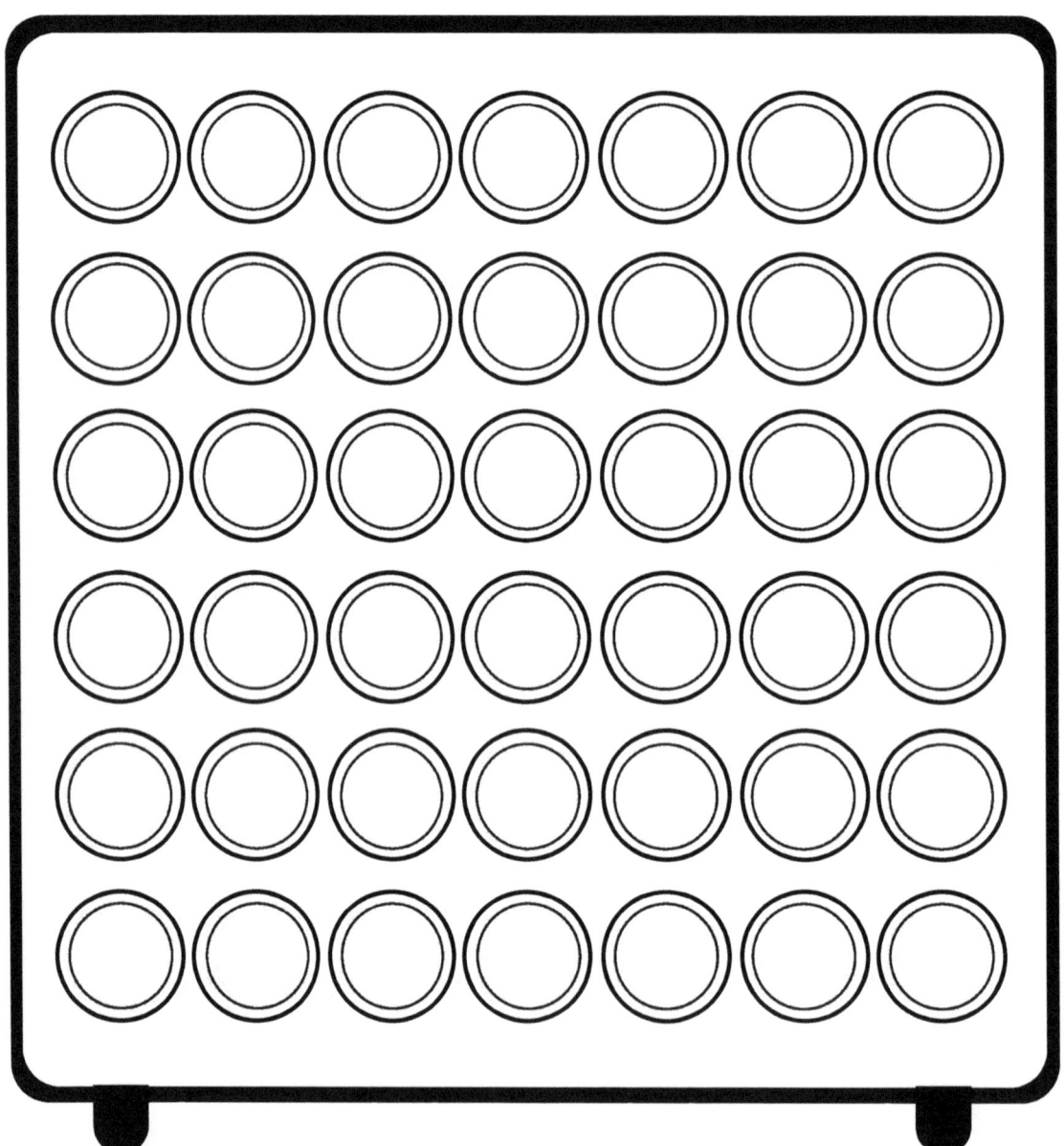

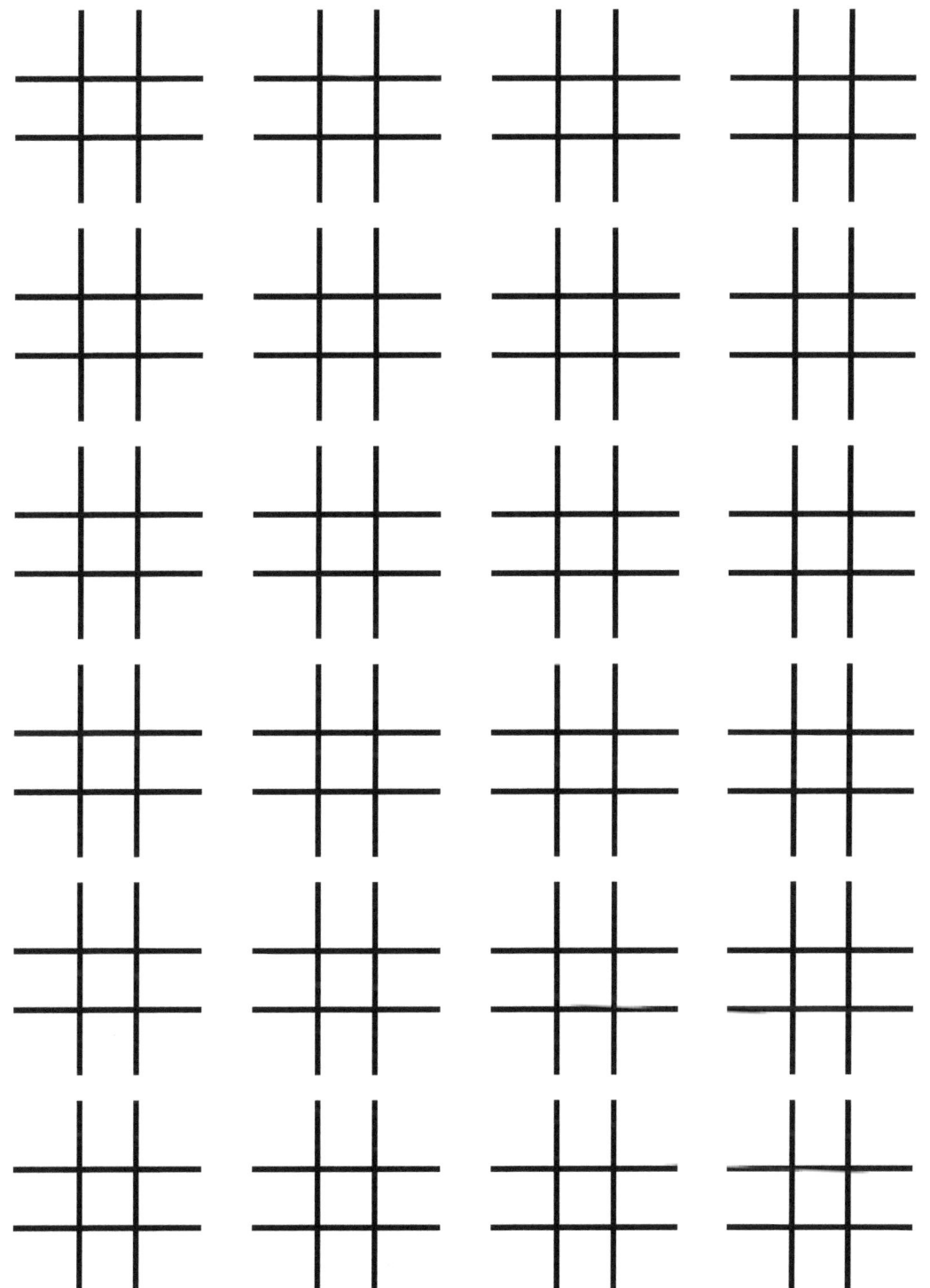

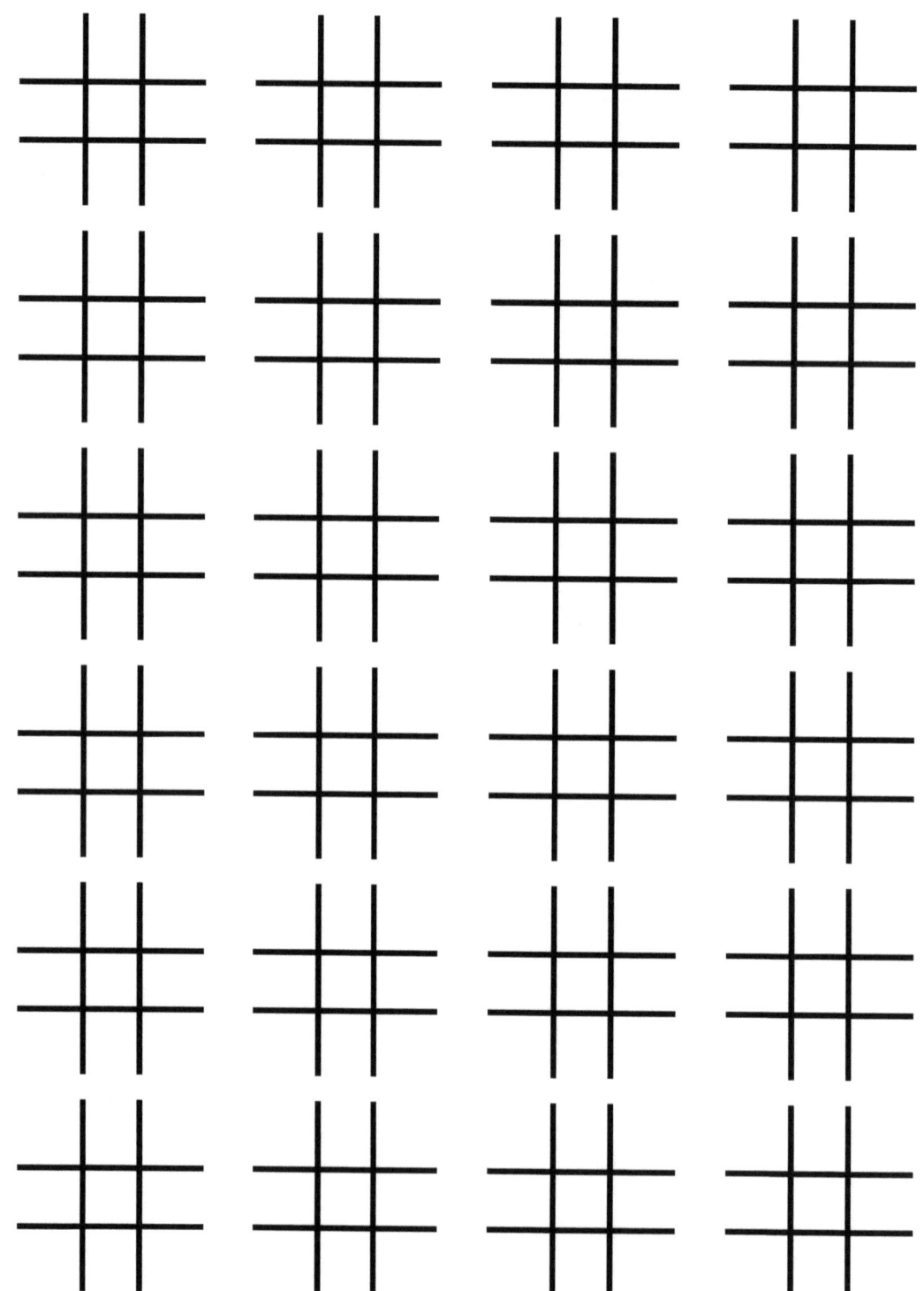

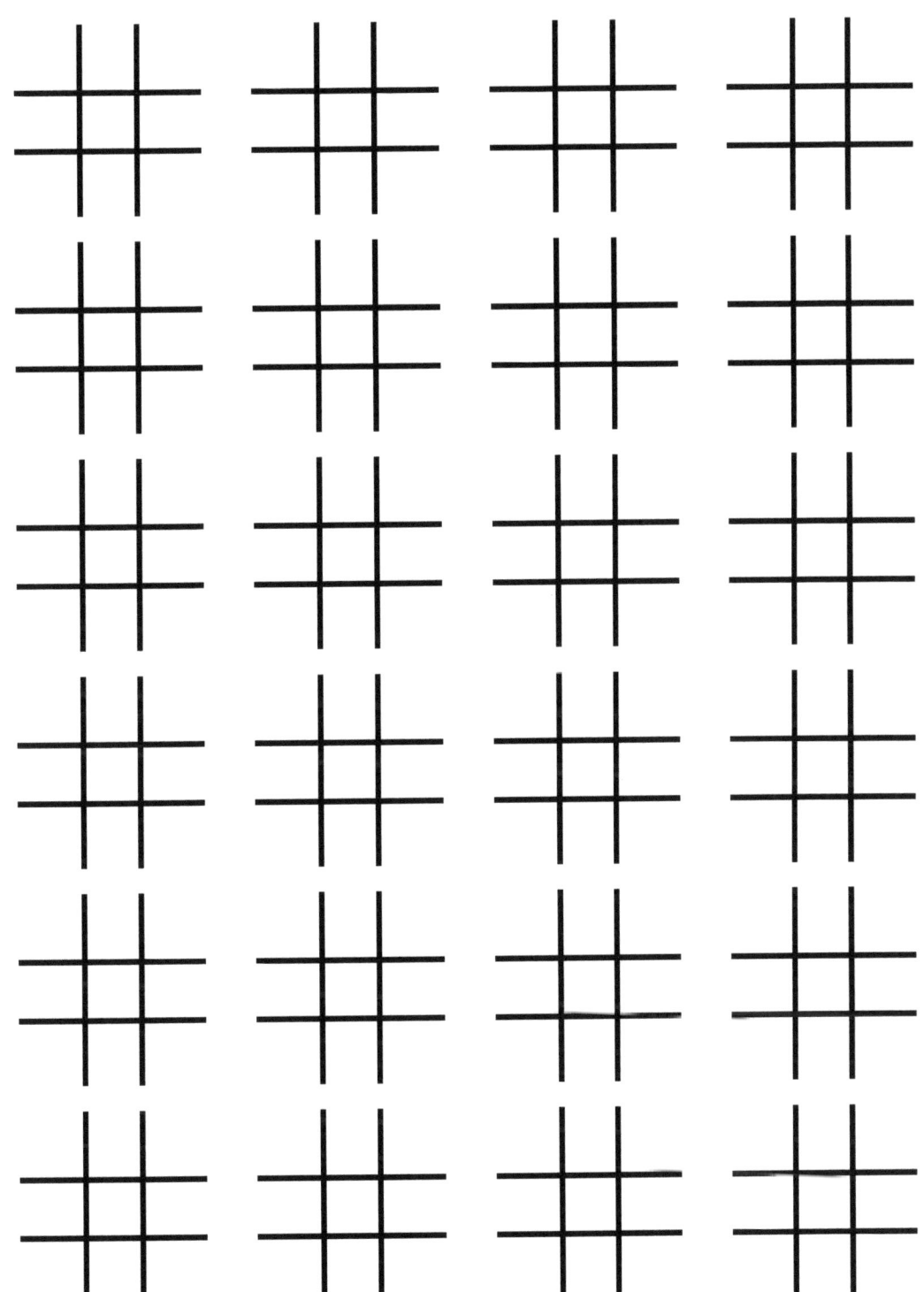

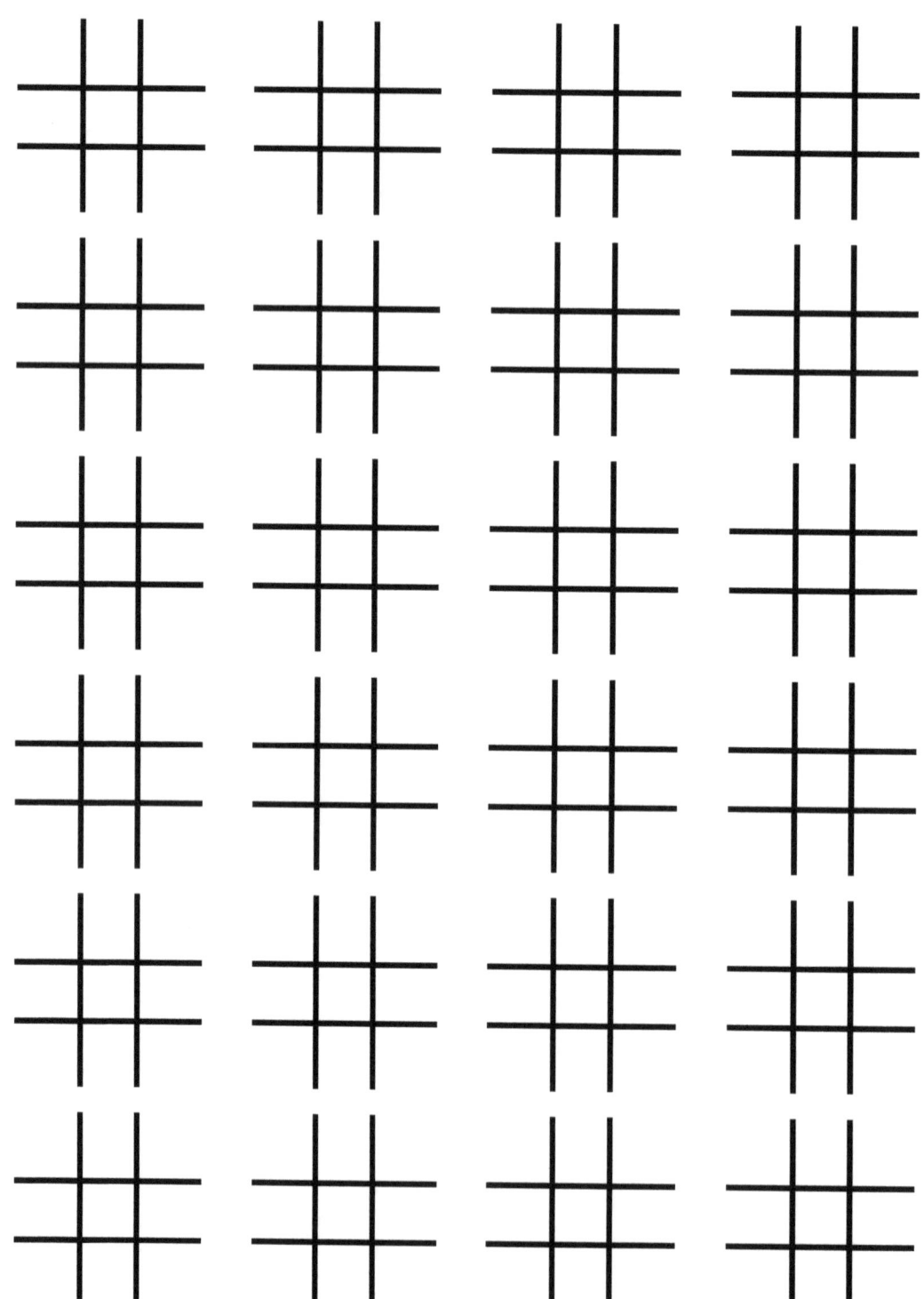

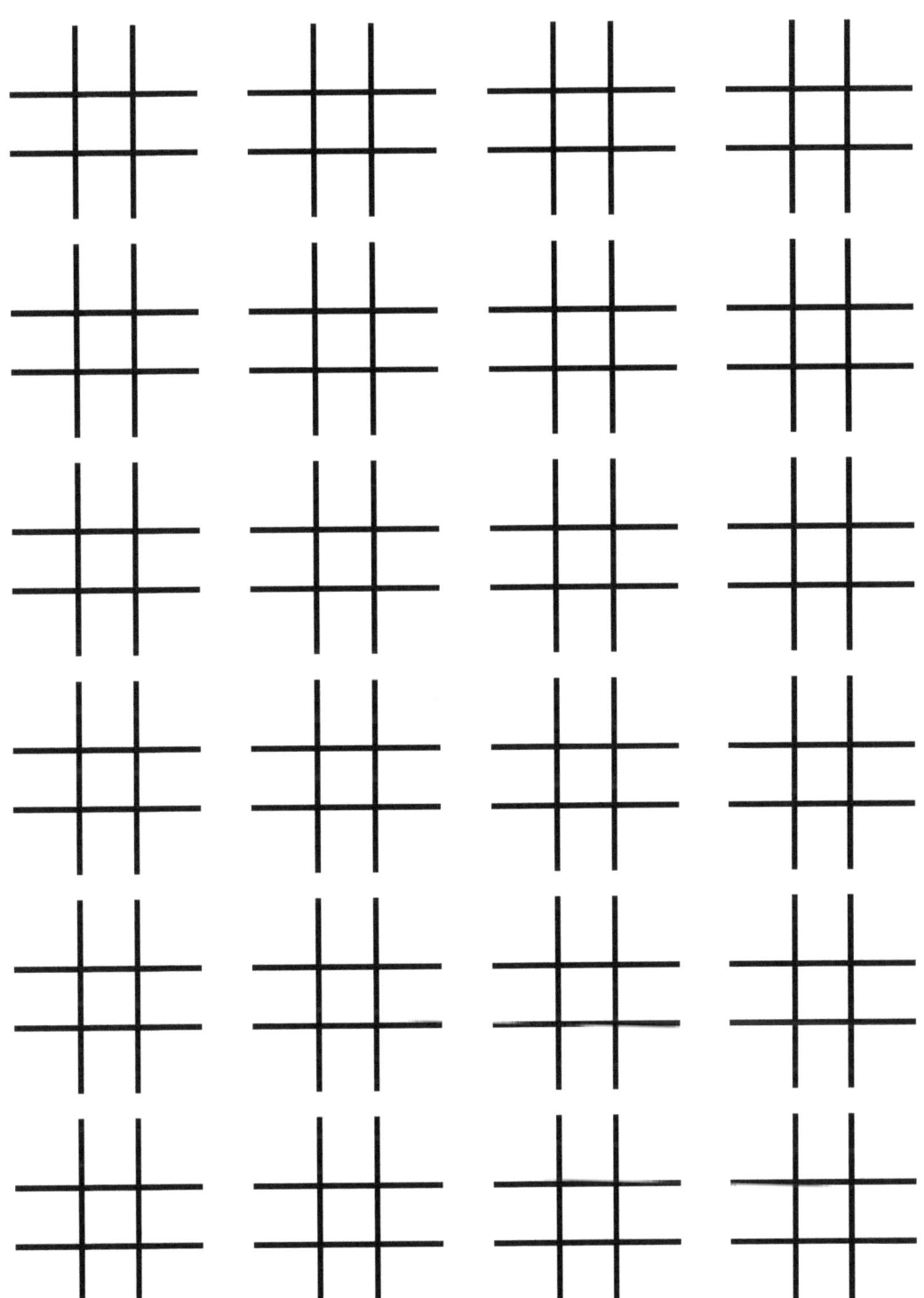

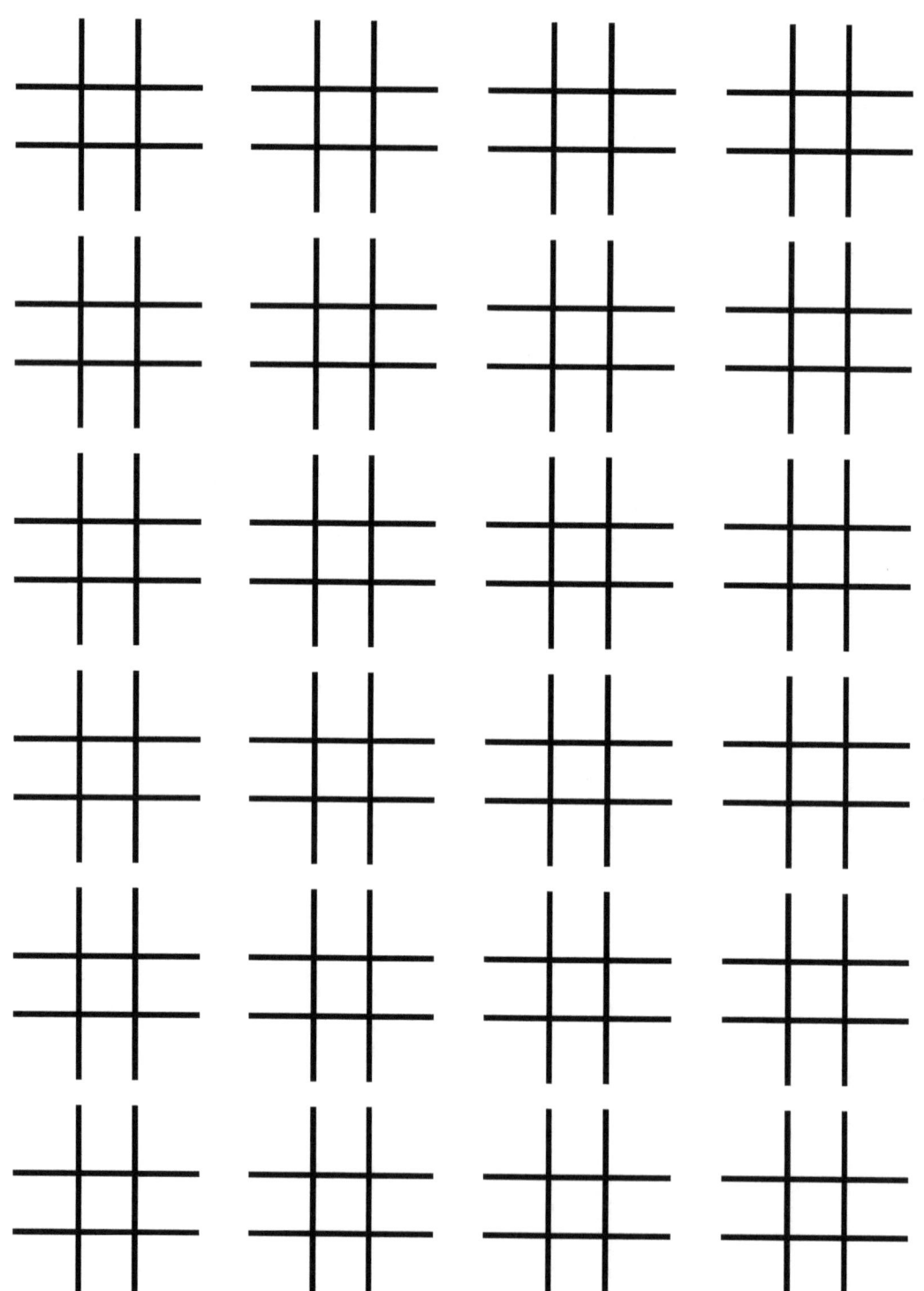

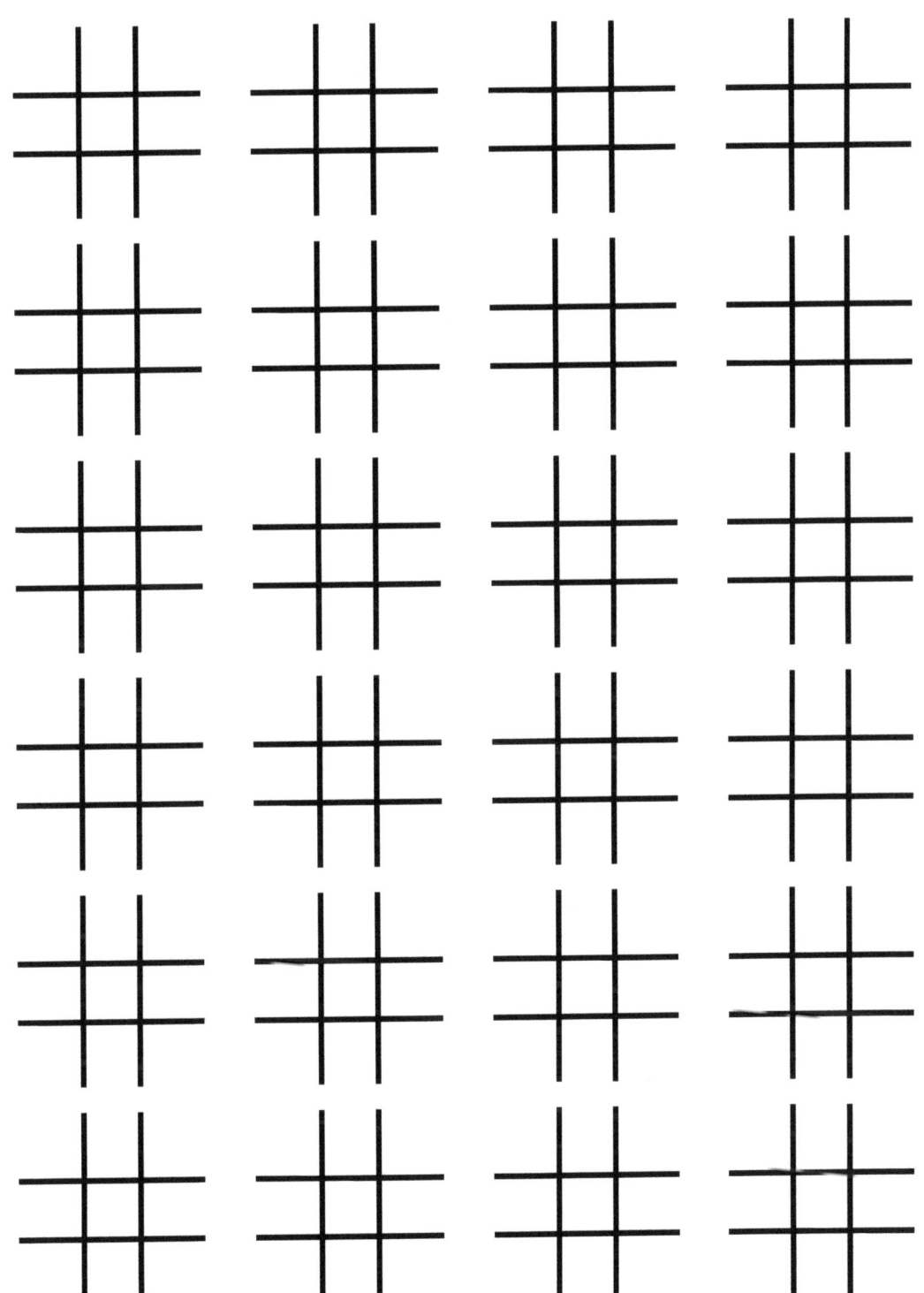

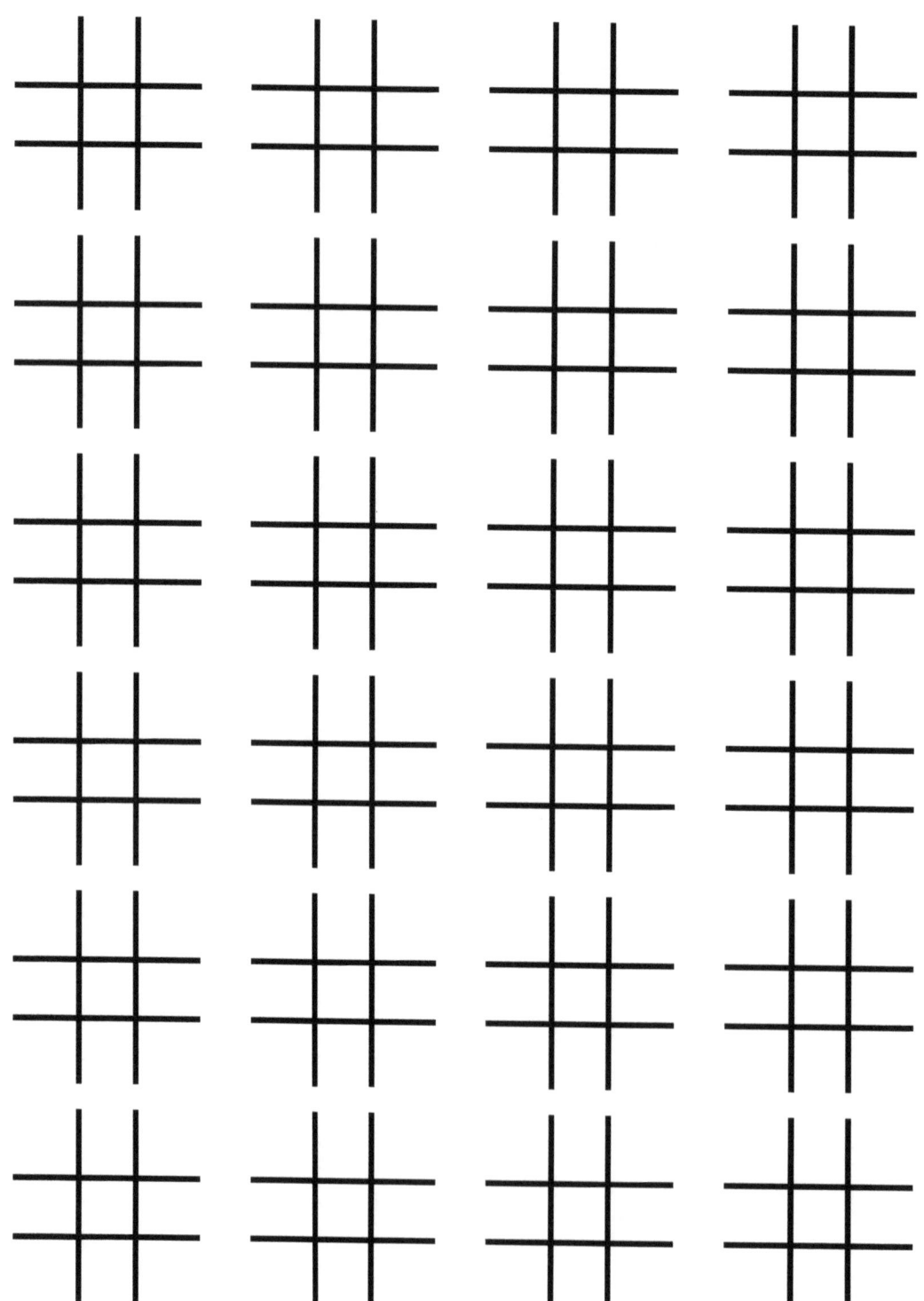

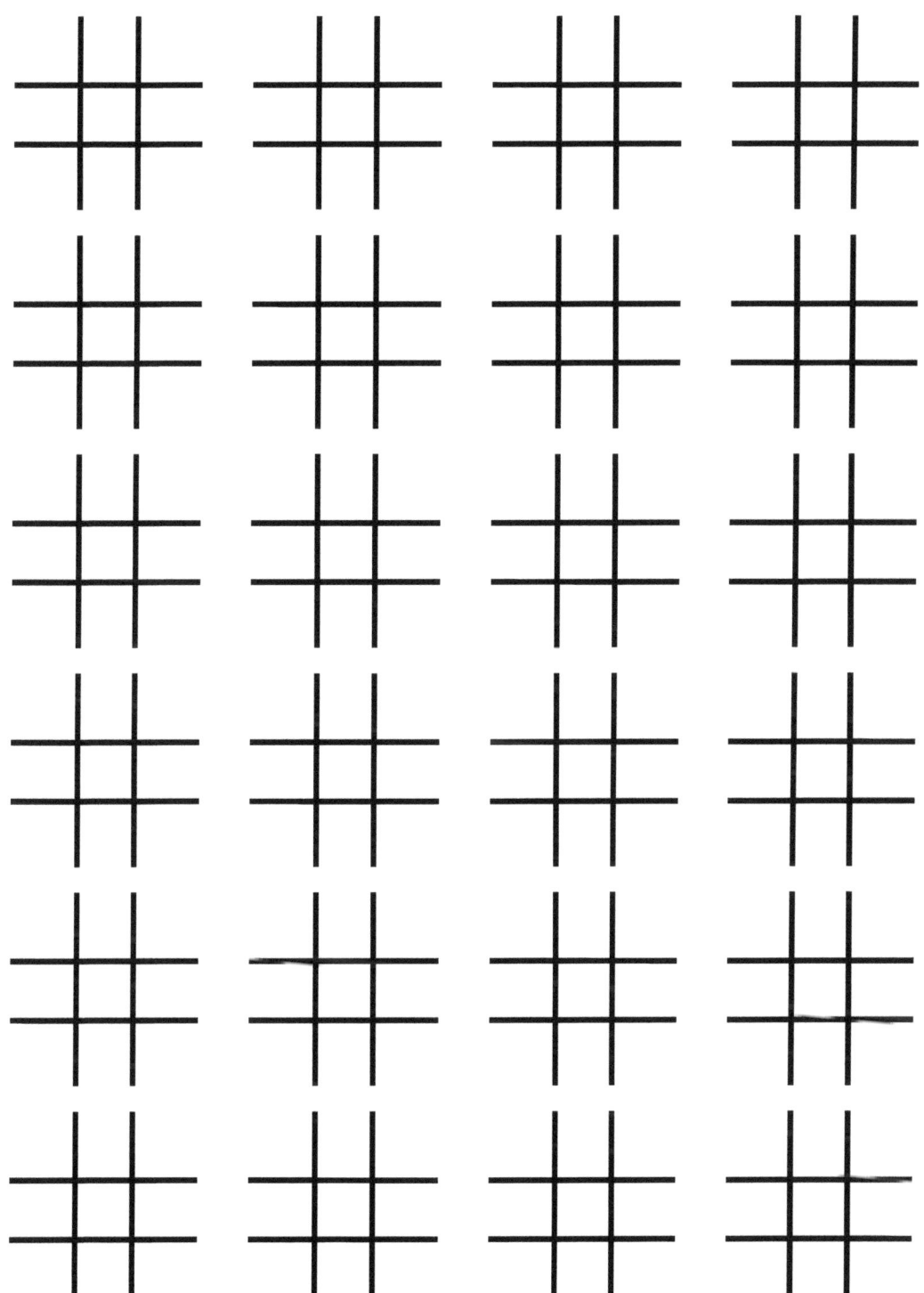

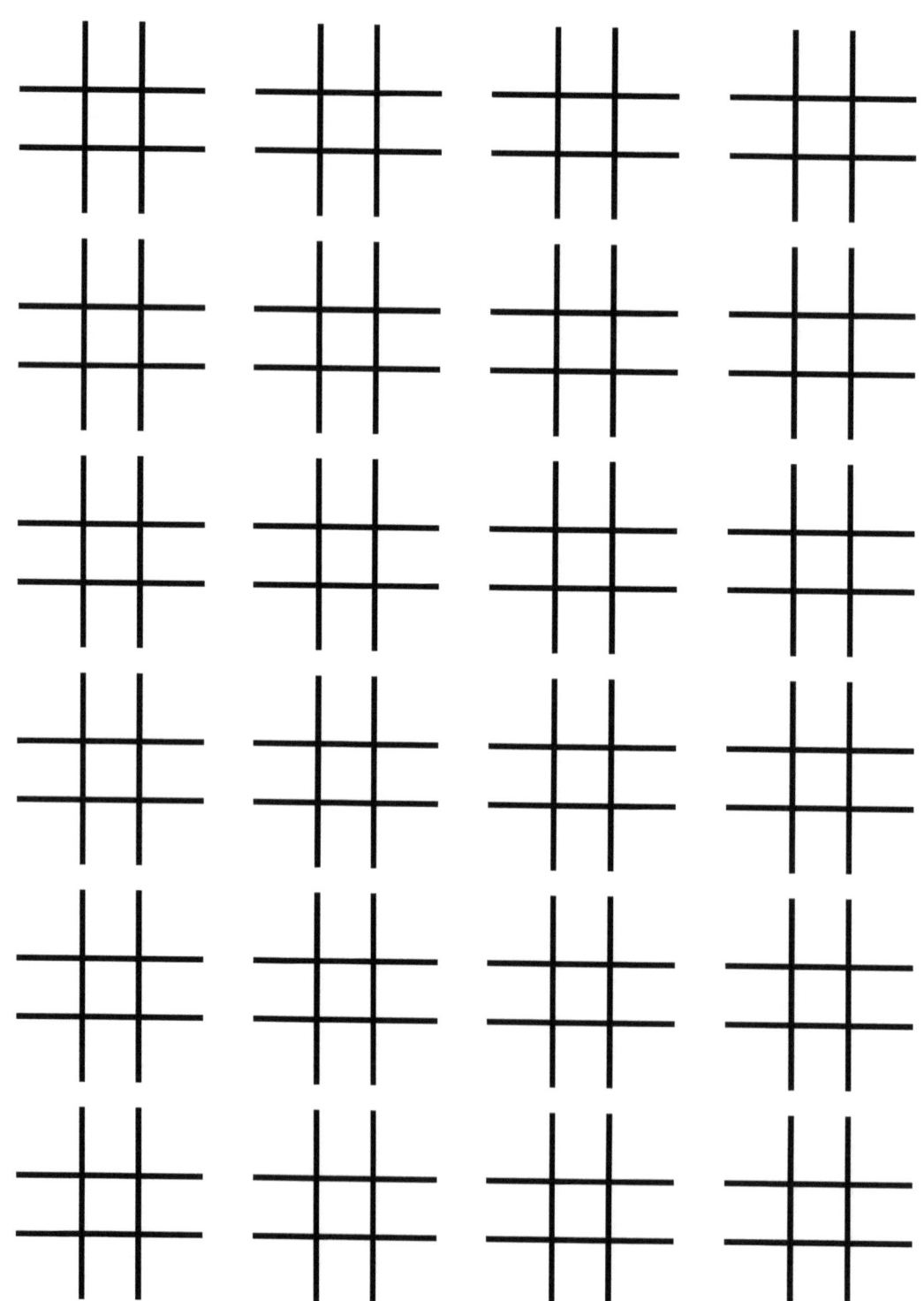

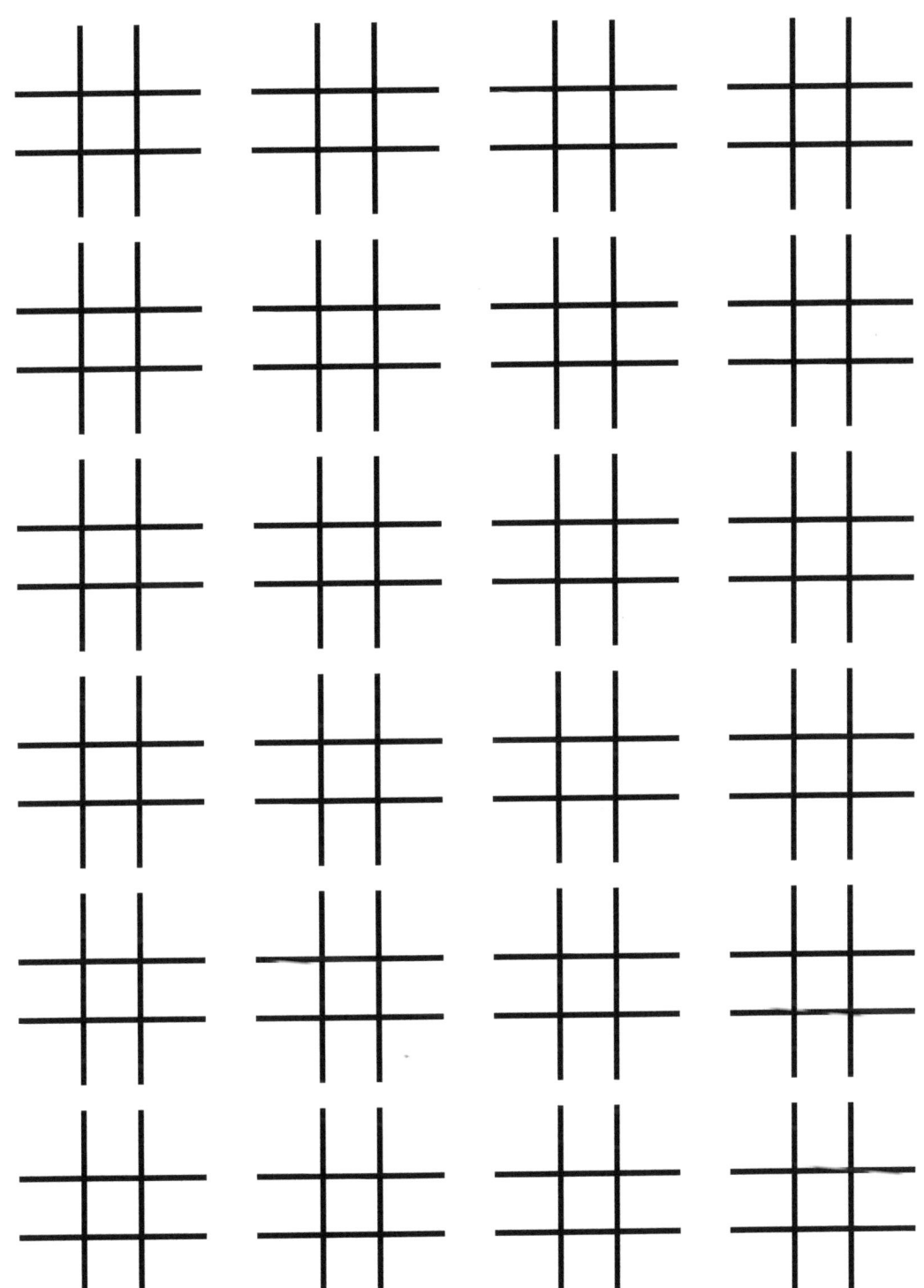

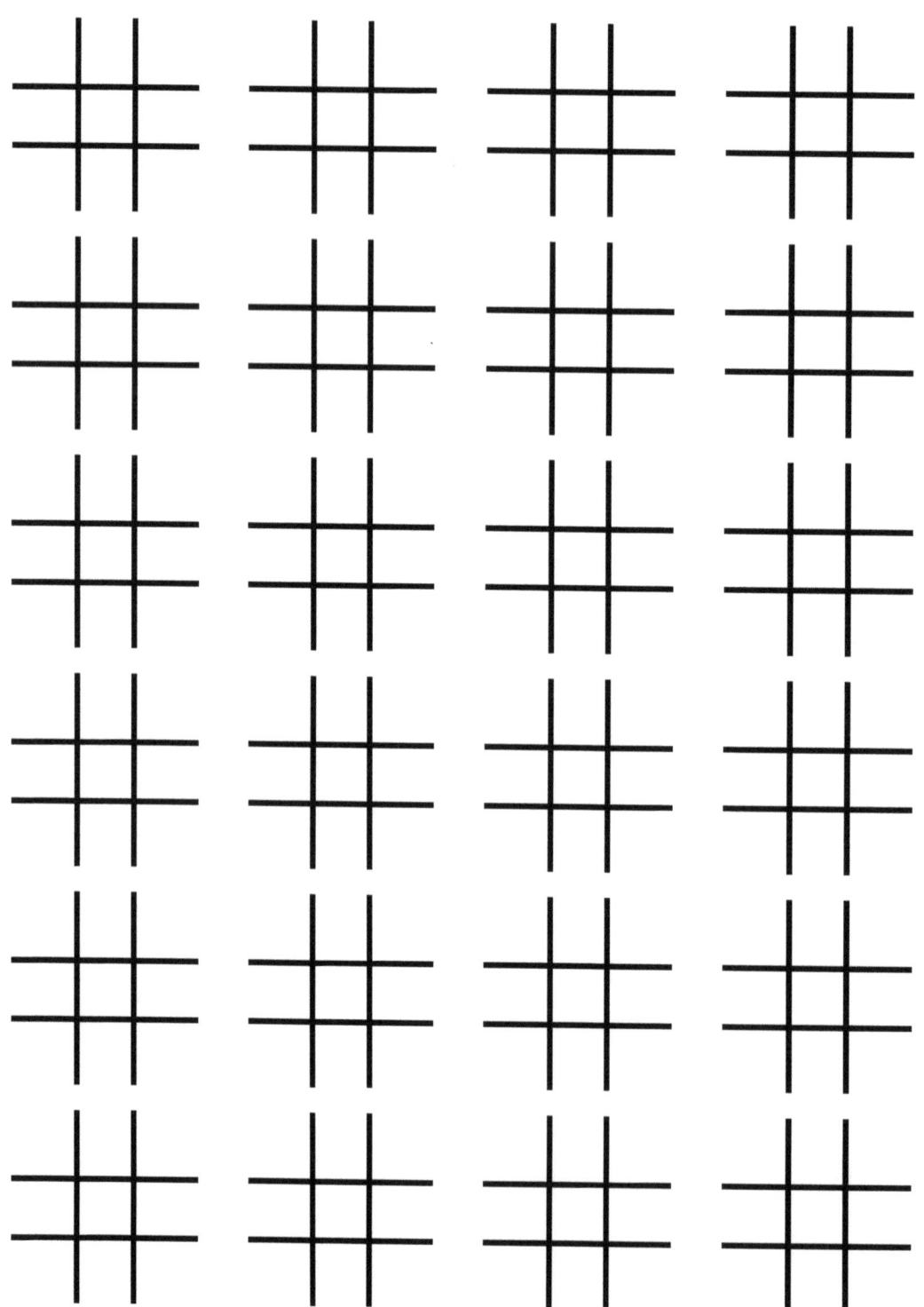

ABCDEFGHIJKLMN
OPQRSTUVWXYZ

_ _ _ _ _ _ _ _ _ _ _ _ _ _ _

_ _ _ _ _ _ _ _ _ _ _ _ _ _ _

_ _ _ _ _ _ _ _ _ _ _ _ _ _ _

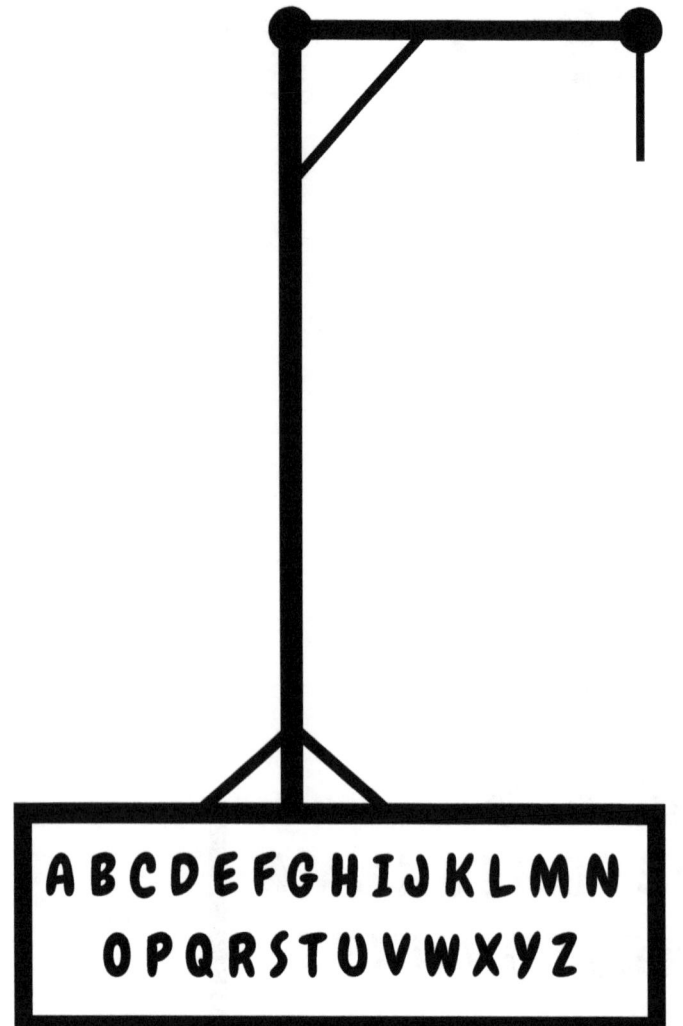

A B C D E F G H I J K L M N
O P Q R S T U V W X Y Z

___ ___ ___ ___ ___ ___ ___ ___ ___ ___

___ ___ ___ ___ ___ ___ ___ ___ ___ ___

___ ___ ___ ___ ___ ___ ___ ___ ___

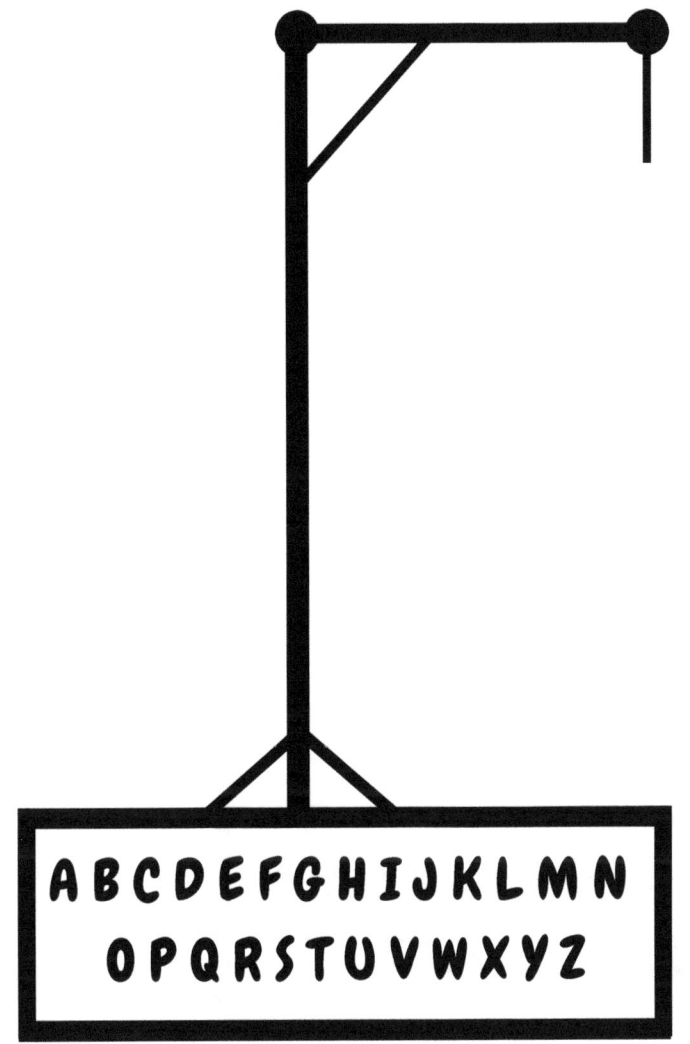

ABCDEFGHIJKLMN
OPQRSTUVWXYZ

_ _ _ _ _ _ _ _ _ _ _ _ _ _

_ _ _ _ _ _ _ _ _ _ _ _ _ _

_ _ _ _ _ _ _ _ _ _ _ _ _ _

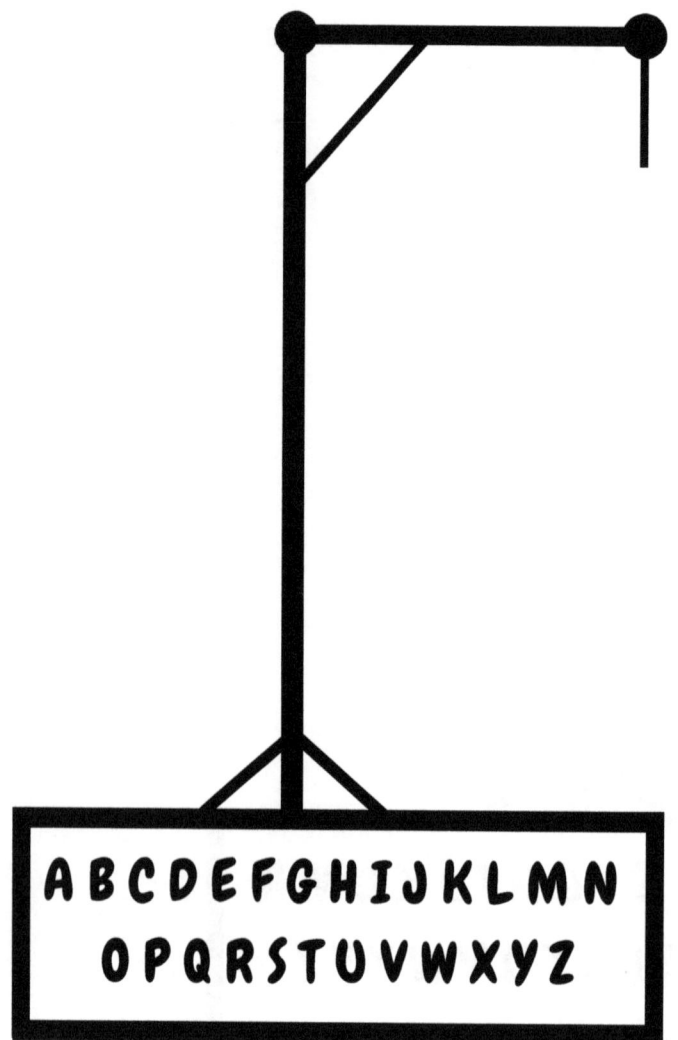

ABCDEFGHIJKLMN
OPQRSTUVWXYZ

_ _ _ _ _ _ _ _ _ _ _ _ _ _

_ _ _ _ _ _ _ _ _ _ _ _ _ _

_ _ _ _ _ _ _ _ _ _ _ _ _ _

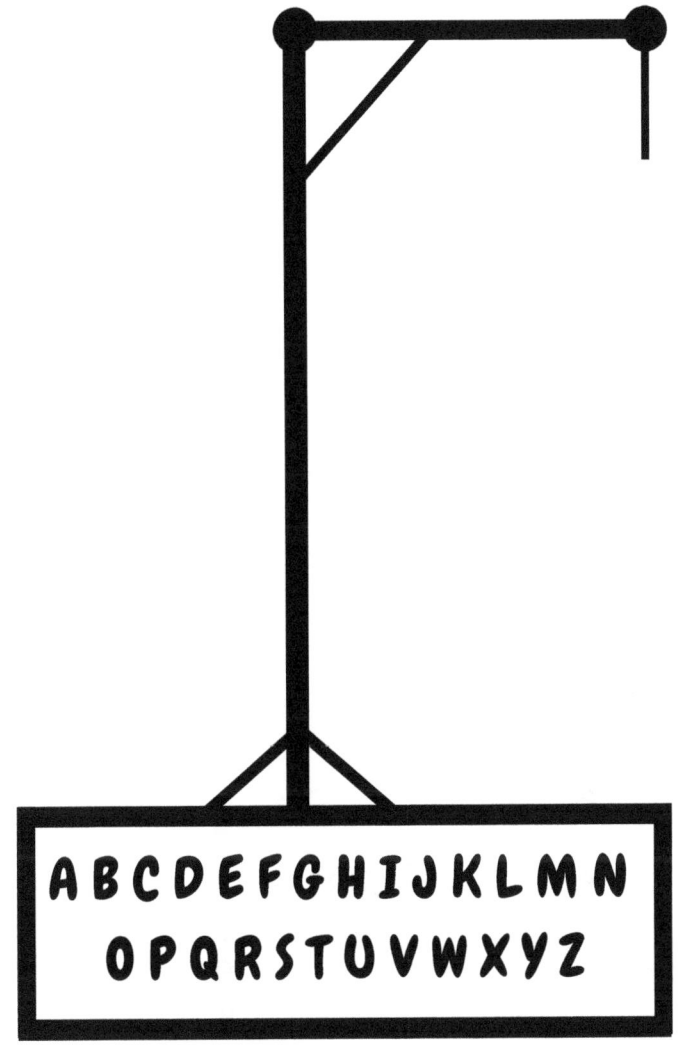

ABCDEFGHIJKLMN
OPQRSTUVWXYZ

_ _ _ _ _ _ _ _ _ _ _ _ _ _ _ _

_ _ _ _ _ _ _ _ _ _ _ _ _ _ _ _

_ _ _ _ _ _ _ _ _ _ _ _ _ _ _ _

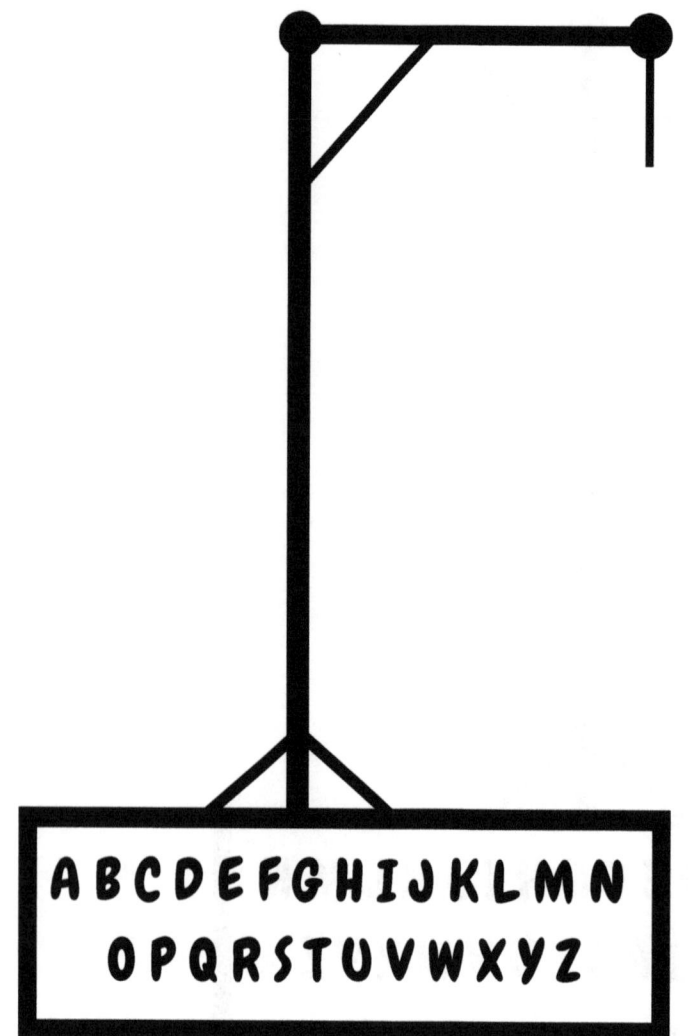

ABCDEFGHIJKLMN
OPQRSTUVWXYZ

- - - - - - - - - - - - - -

- - - - - - - - - - - - - -

- - - - - - - - - - - - - -

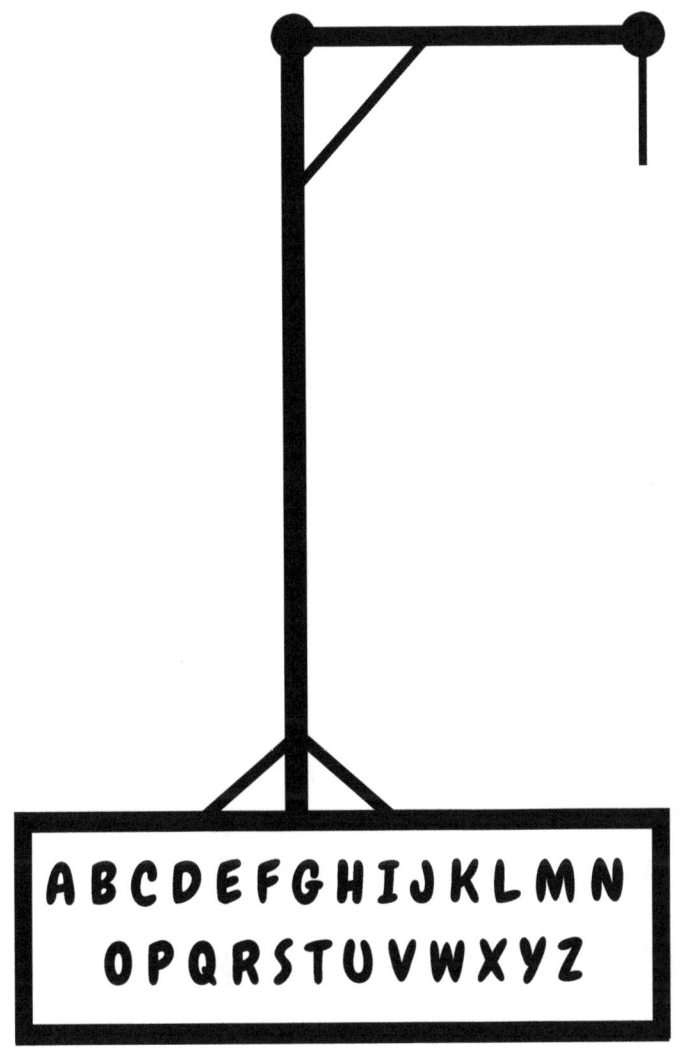

ABCDEFGHIJKLMN
OPQRSTUVWXYZ

- - - - - - - - - - - - - - - -

- - - - - - - - - - - - - - - -

- - - - - - - - - - - - - - - -

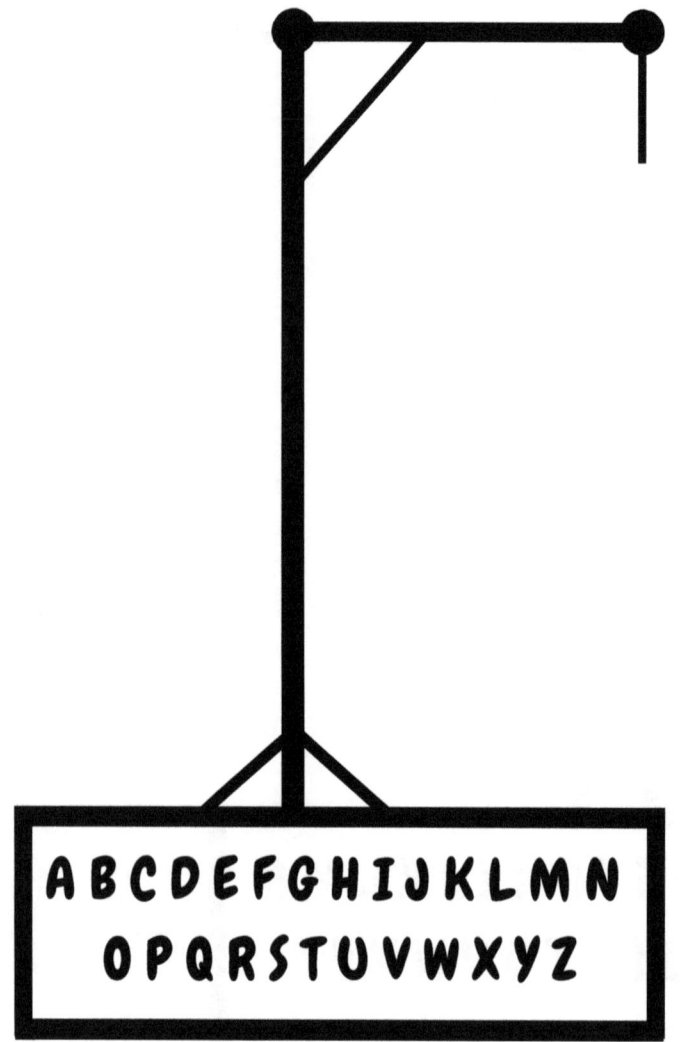

ABCDEFGHIJKLMN
OPQRSTUVWXYZ

- - - - - - - - - - - - - - - -

- - - - - - - - - - - - - - - -

- - - - - - - - - - - - - - - -

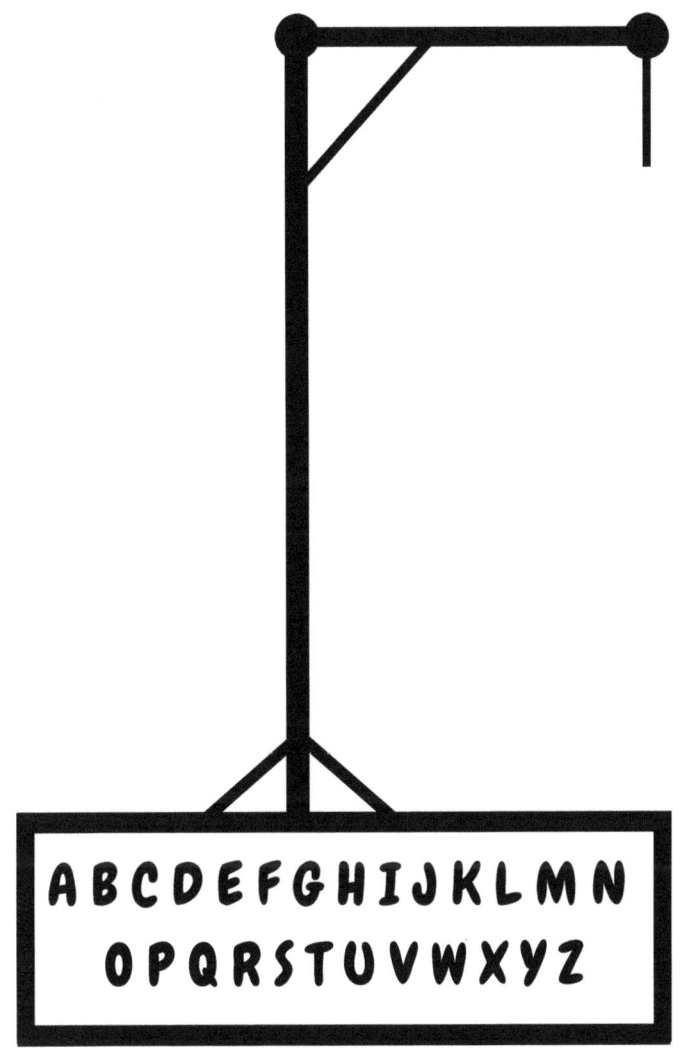

ABCDEFGHIJKLMN
OPQRSTUVWXYZ

_ _

_ _

_ _

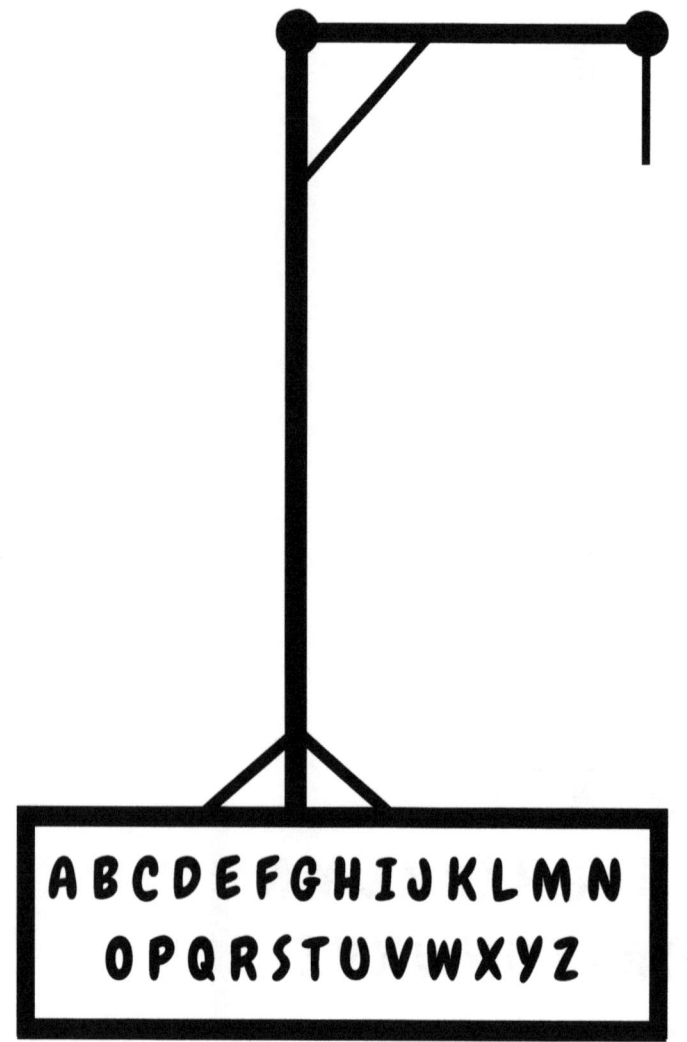

ABCDEFGHIJKLMN
OPQRSTUVWXYZ

- - - - - - - - - - - - - - - -

- - - - - - - - - - - - - - - -

- - - - - - - - - - - - - - - -

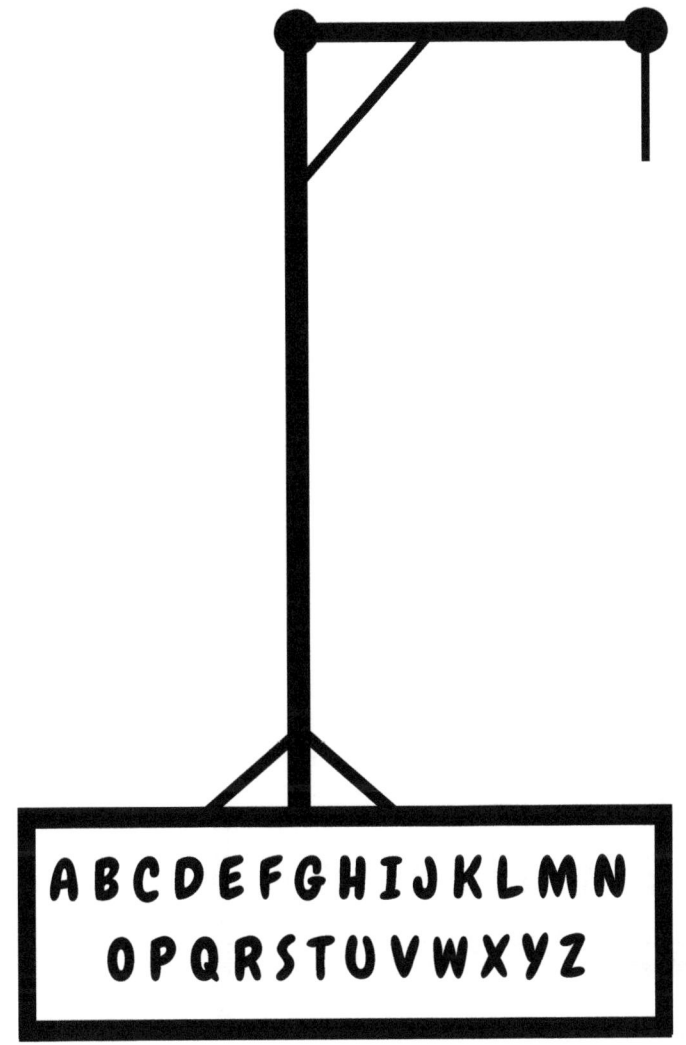

ABCDEFGHIJKLMN
OPQRSTUVWXYZ

- - - - - - - - - - - - - - - -

- - - - - - - - - - - - - - - -

- - - - - - - - - - - - - - - -

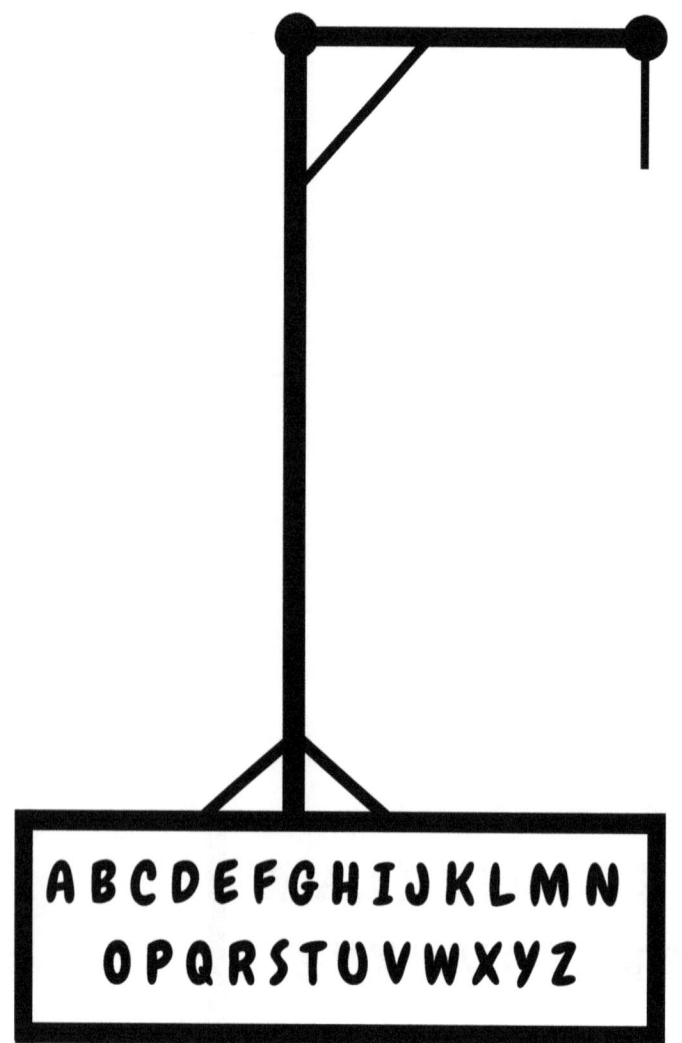

ABCDEFGHIJKLMN
OPQRSTUVWXYZ

- - - - - - - - - - - - - - -

- - - - - - - - - - - - - - -

- - - - - - - - - - - - - - -

CONNECT THE DOTS

CONNECT THE DOTS

CONNECT THE DOTS

CONNECT THE DOTS

CONNECT THE DOTS

CONNECT THE DOTS

CONNECT THE DOTS

CONNECT THE DOTS

CONNECT THE DOTS

CONNECT THE DOTS

CONNECT THE DOTS

CONNECT THE DOTS

LABYRINTH

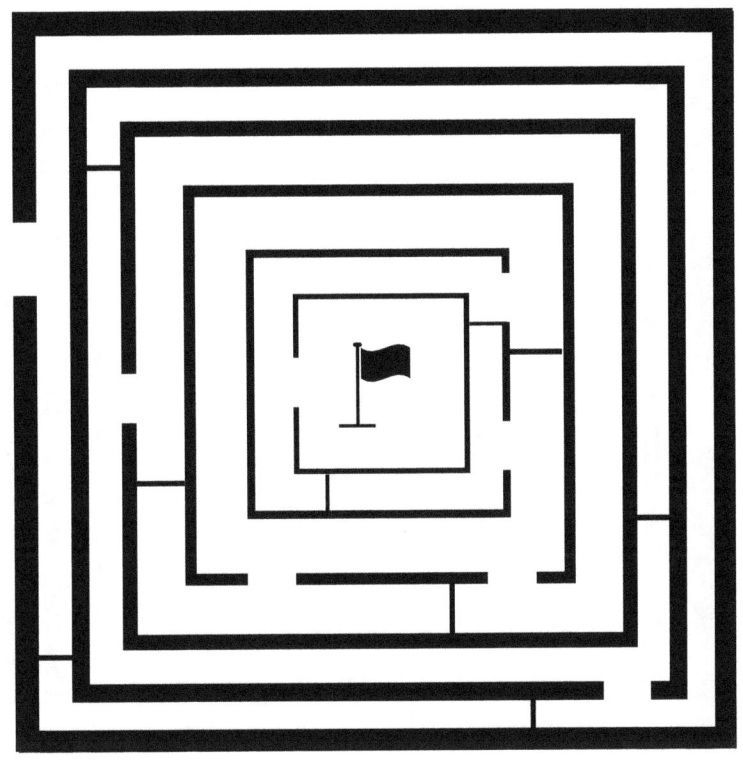

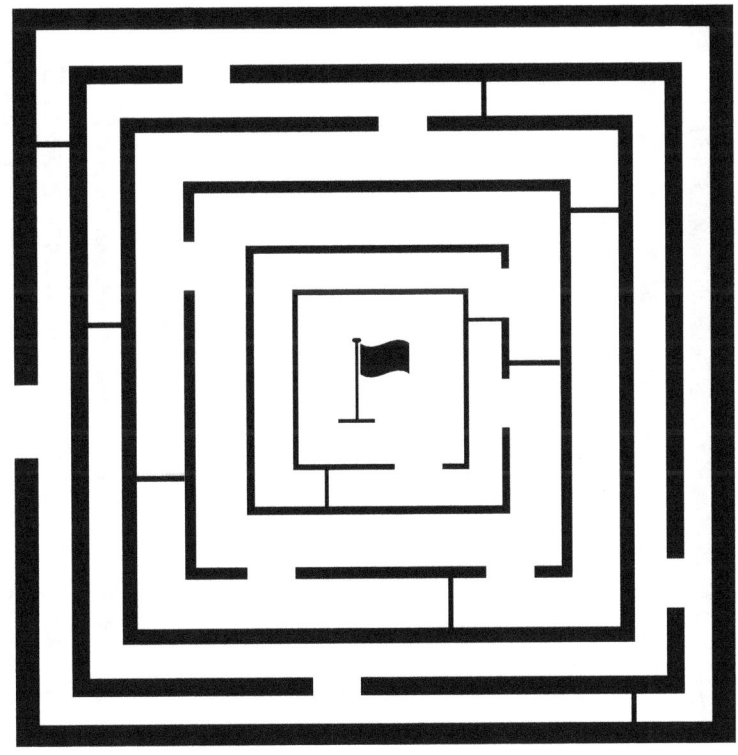

LABYRINTH

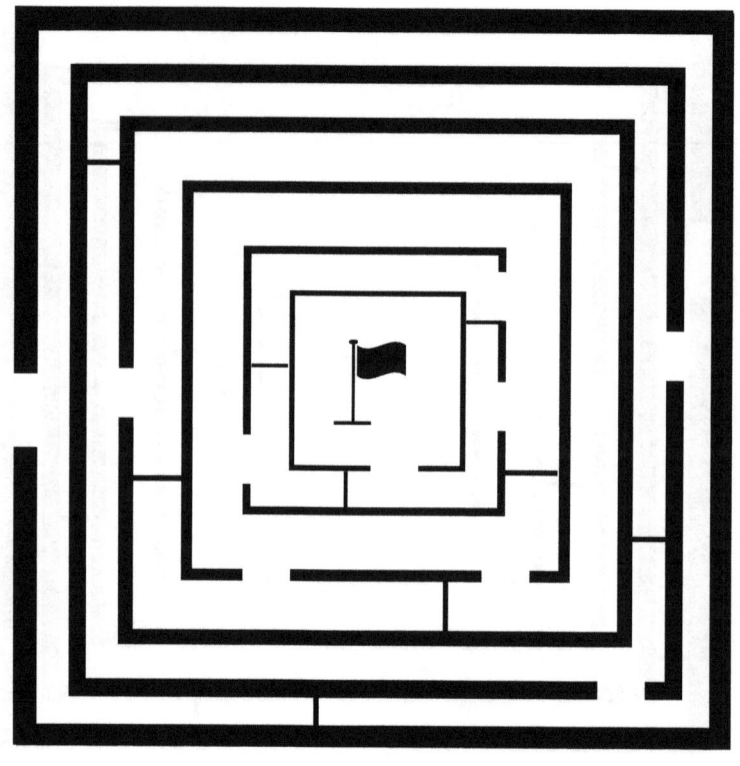

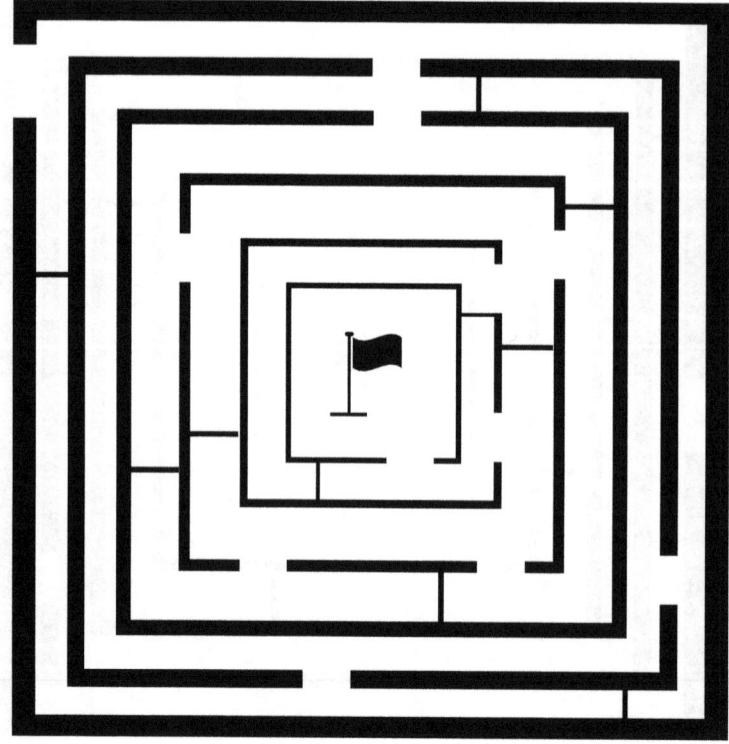

LABYRINTH

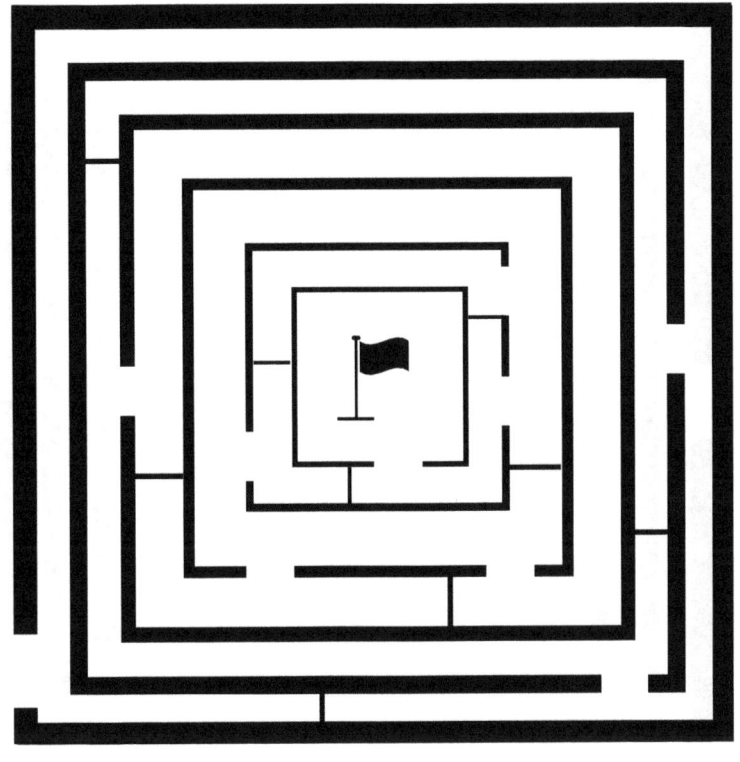

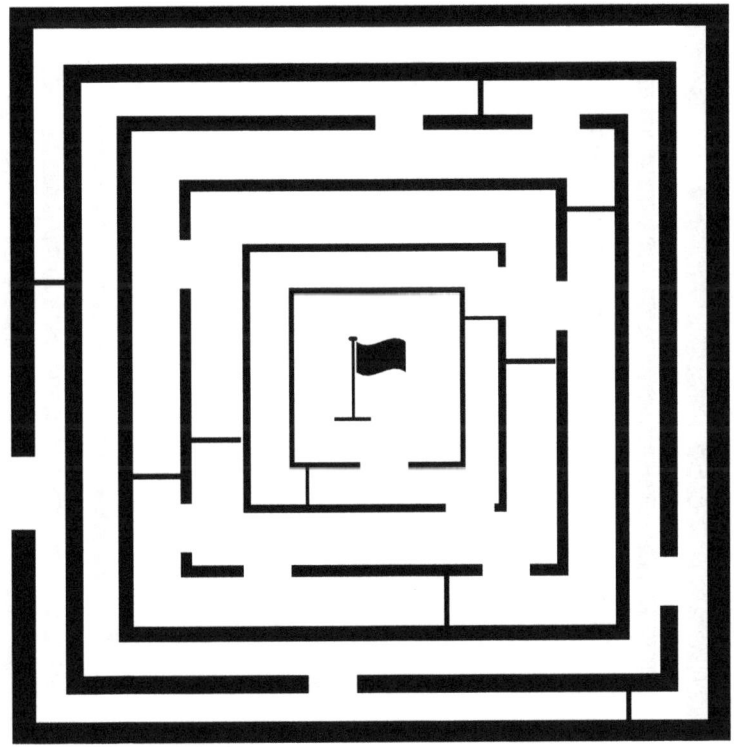

LABYRINTH

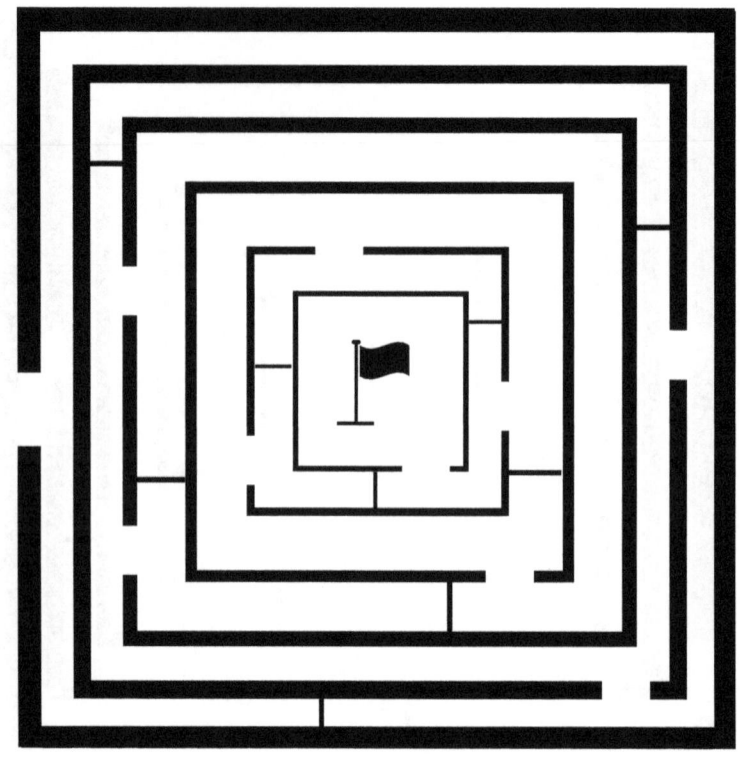

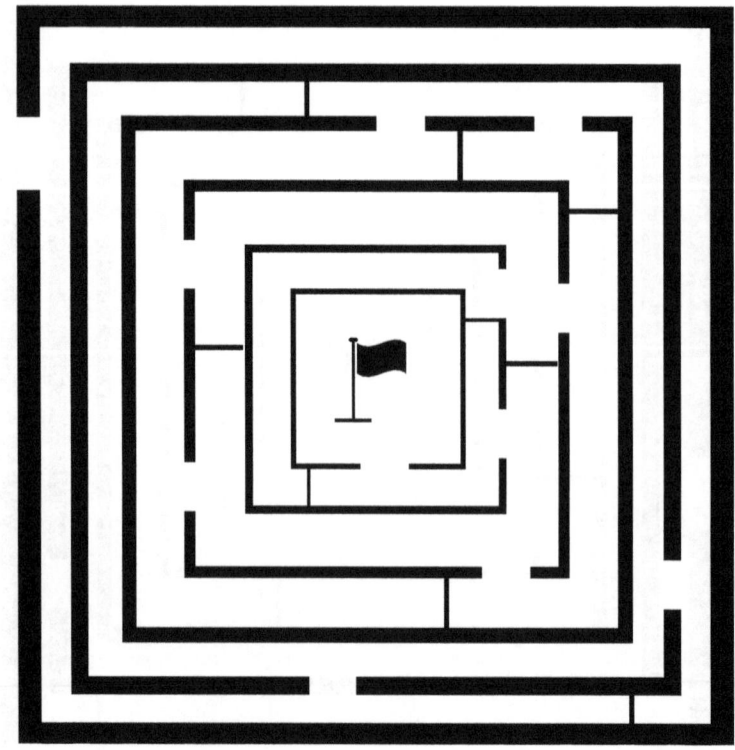

LABYRINTH

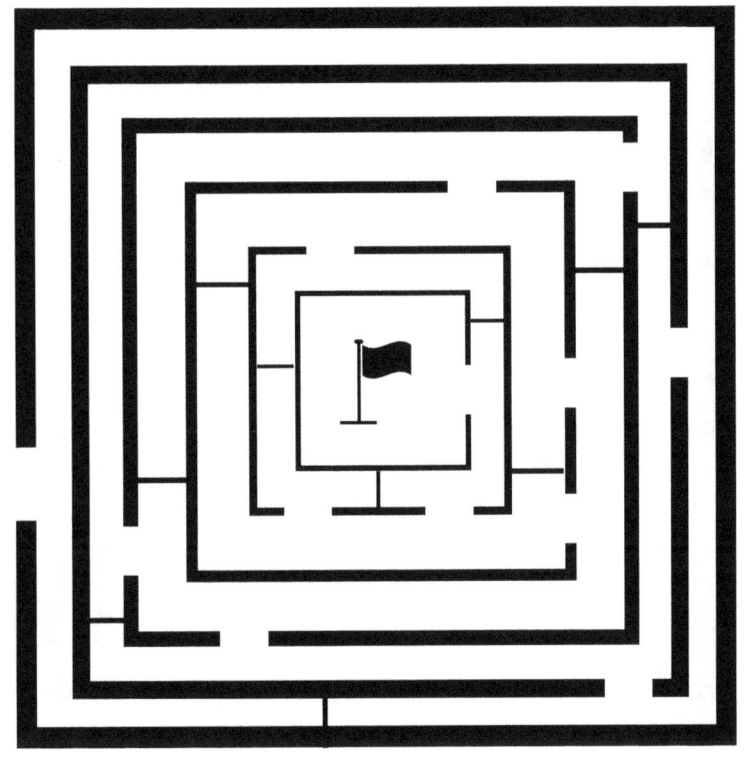

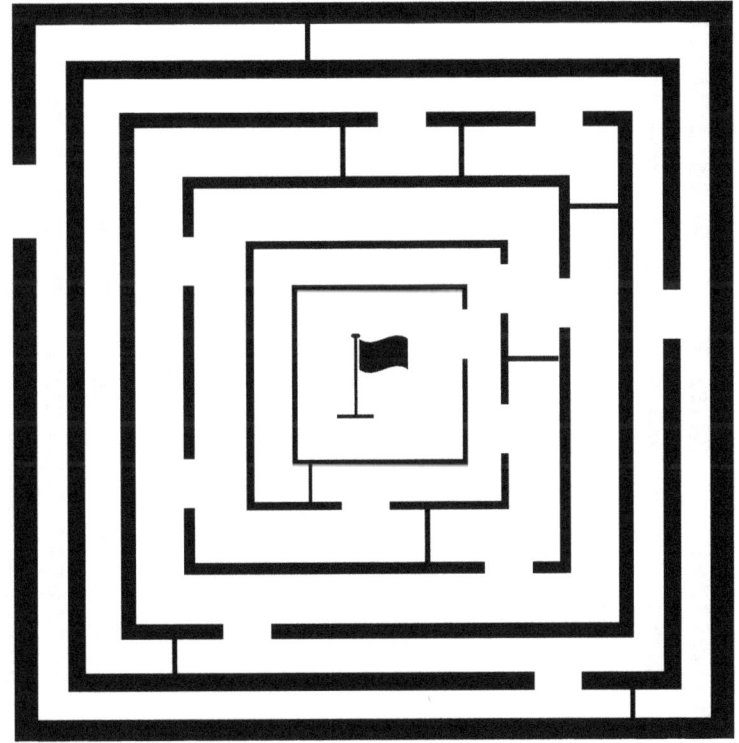

LABYRINTH

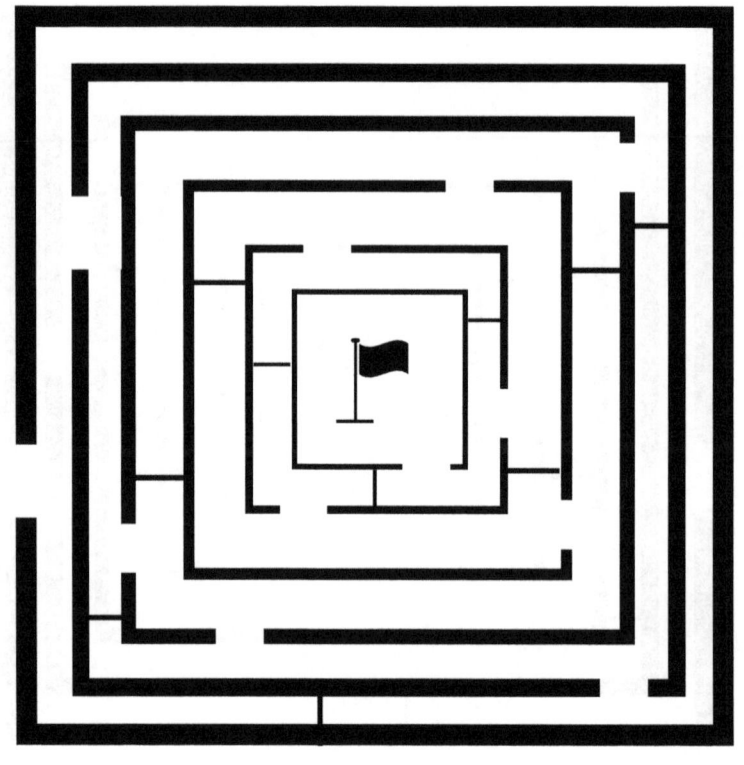

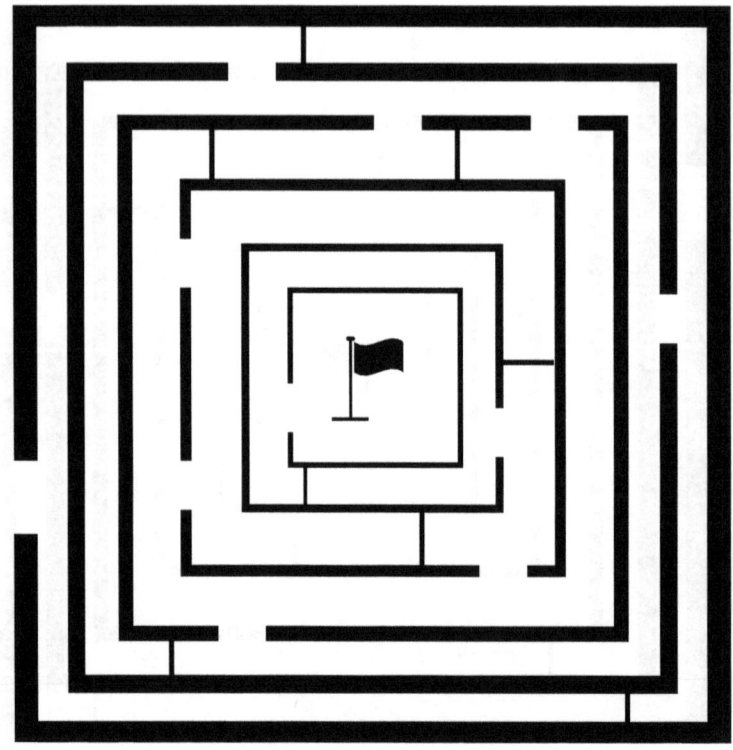

LABYRINTH

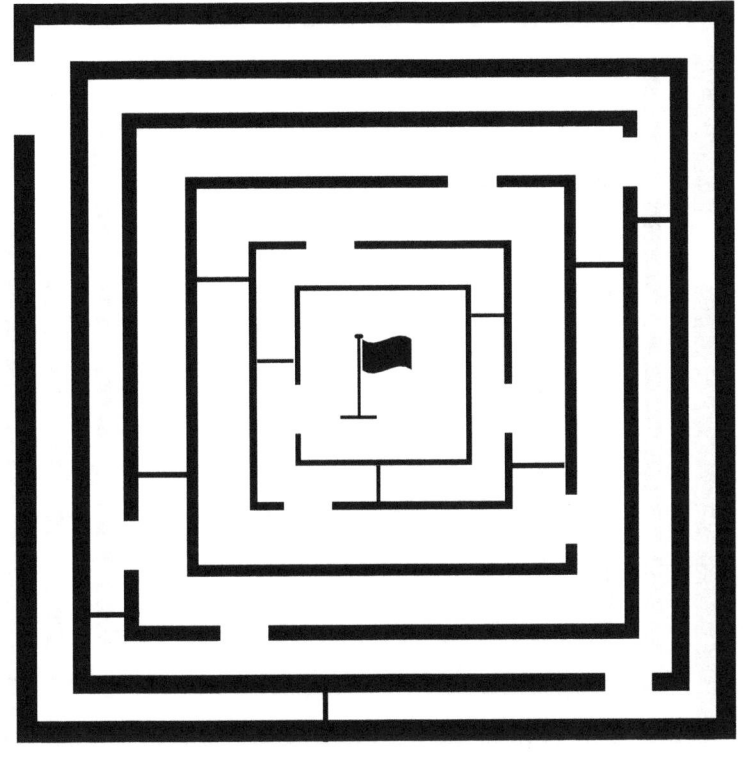

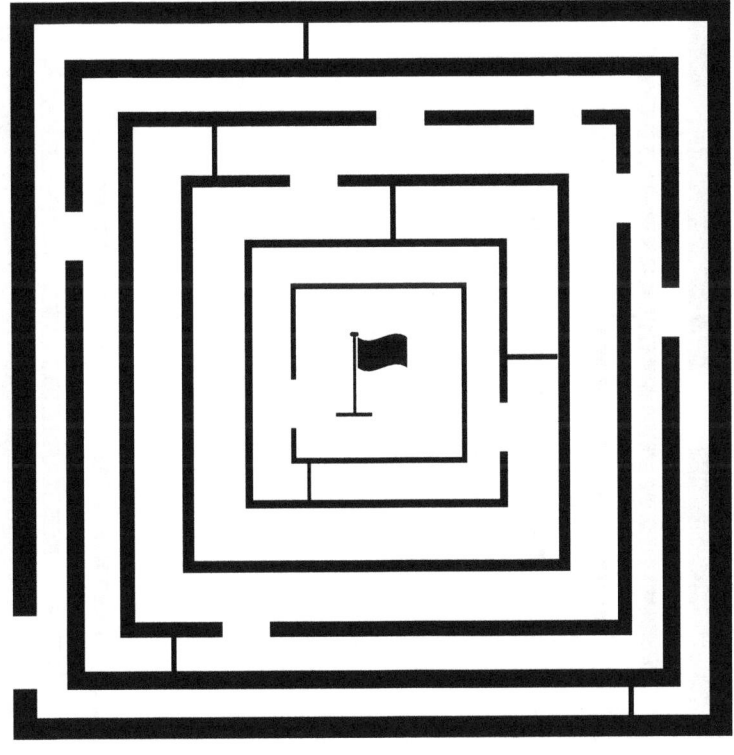

LABYRINTH

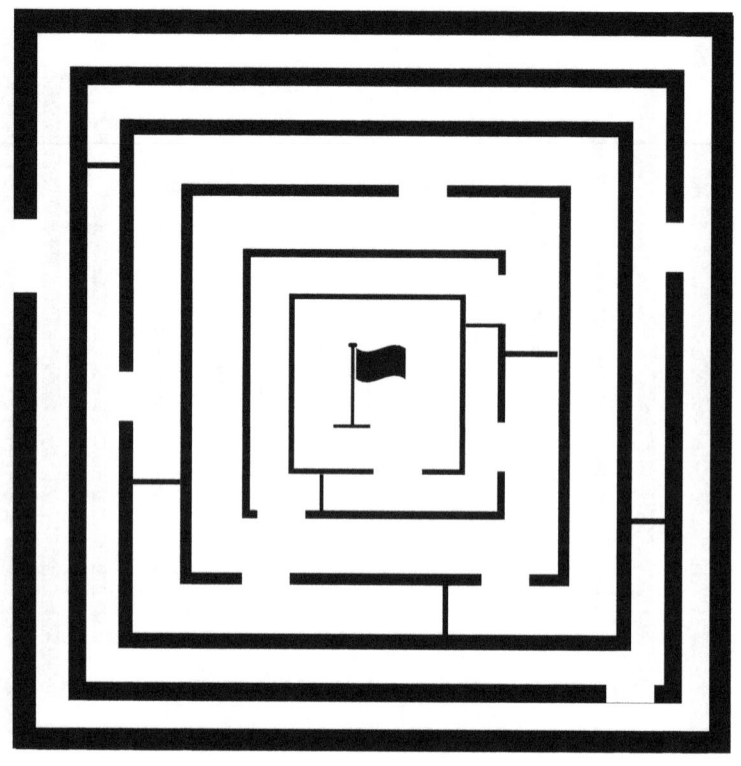

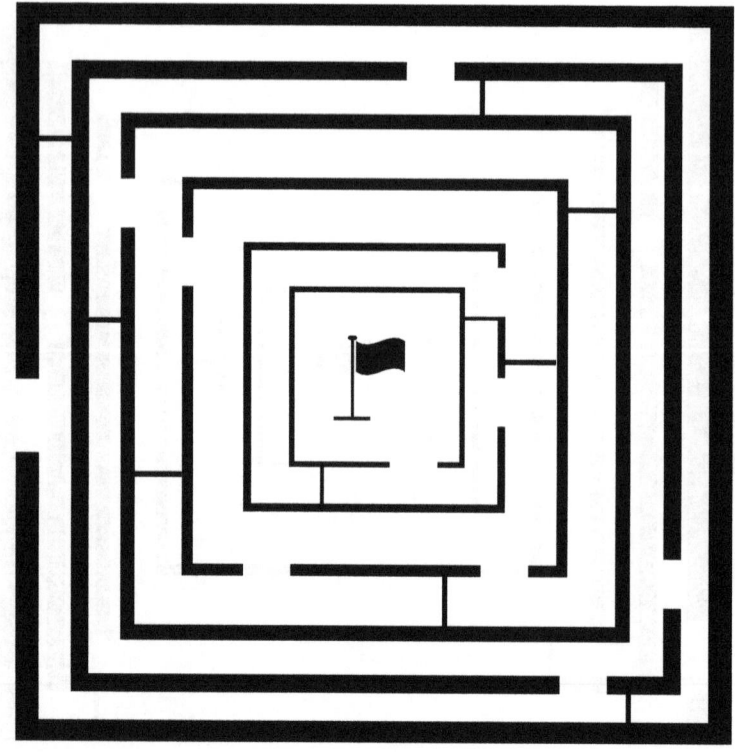

LABYRINTH

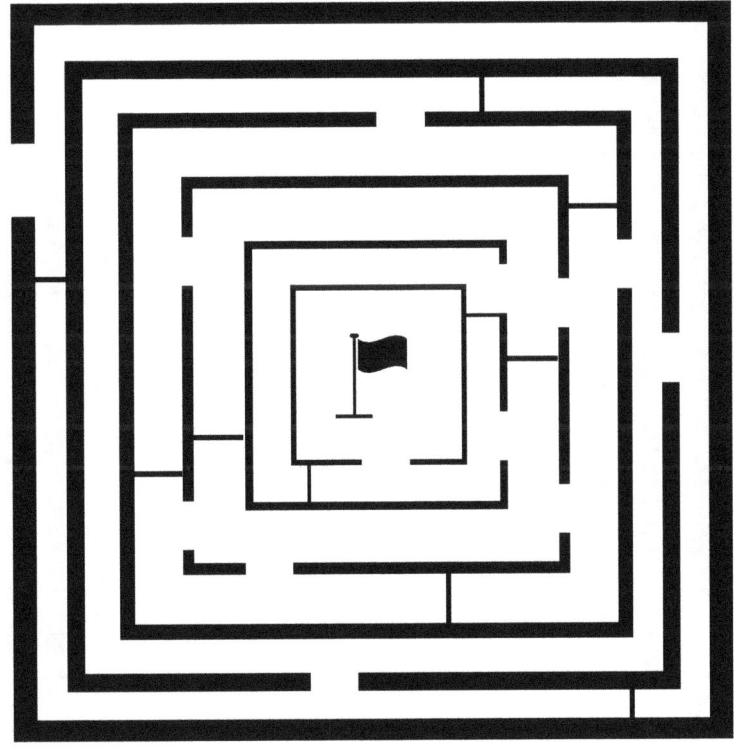

LABYRINTH

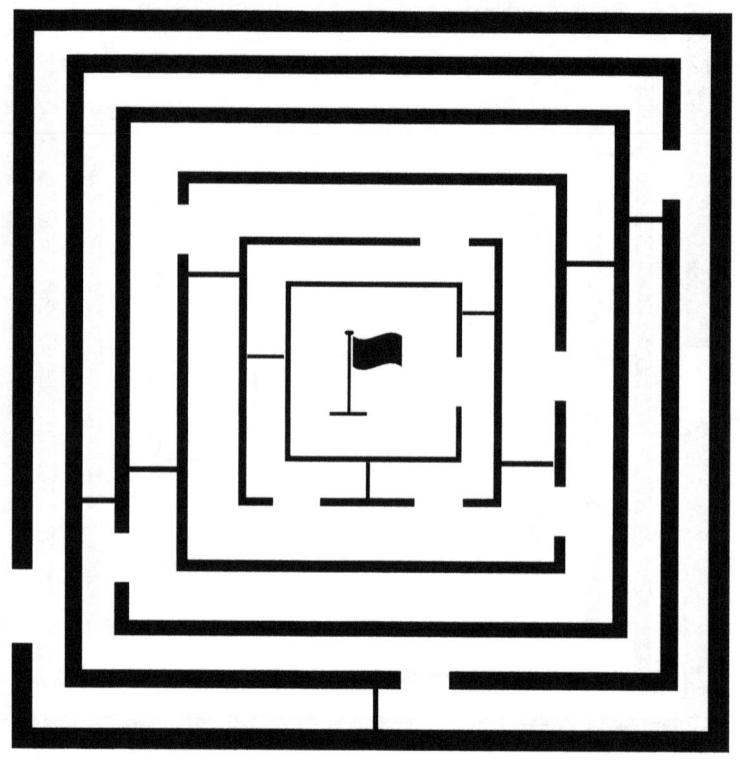

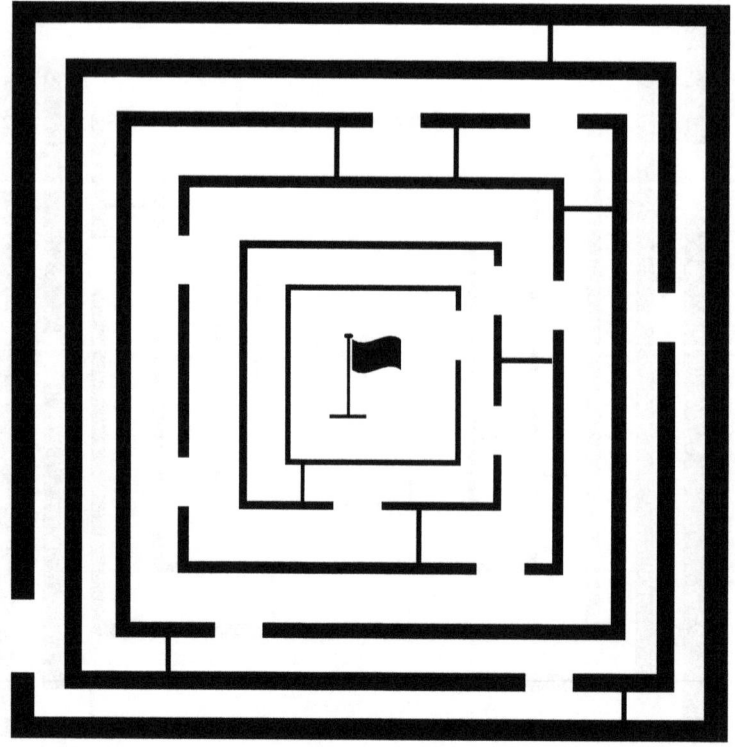

FIND THE SAME SIZE

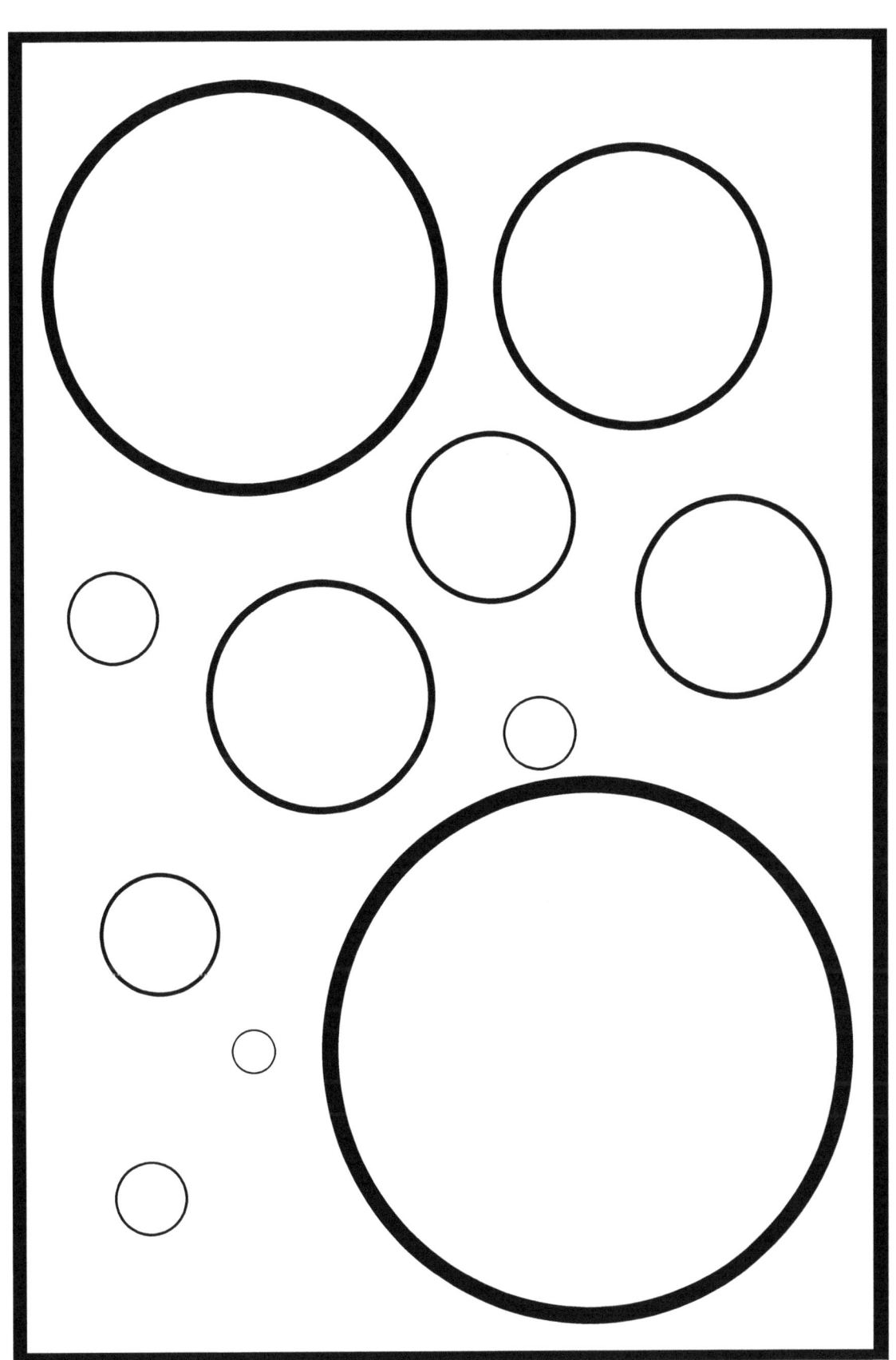

SOLUTION

FIND THE SAME SIZE

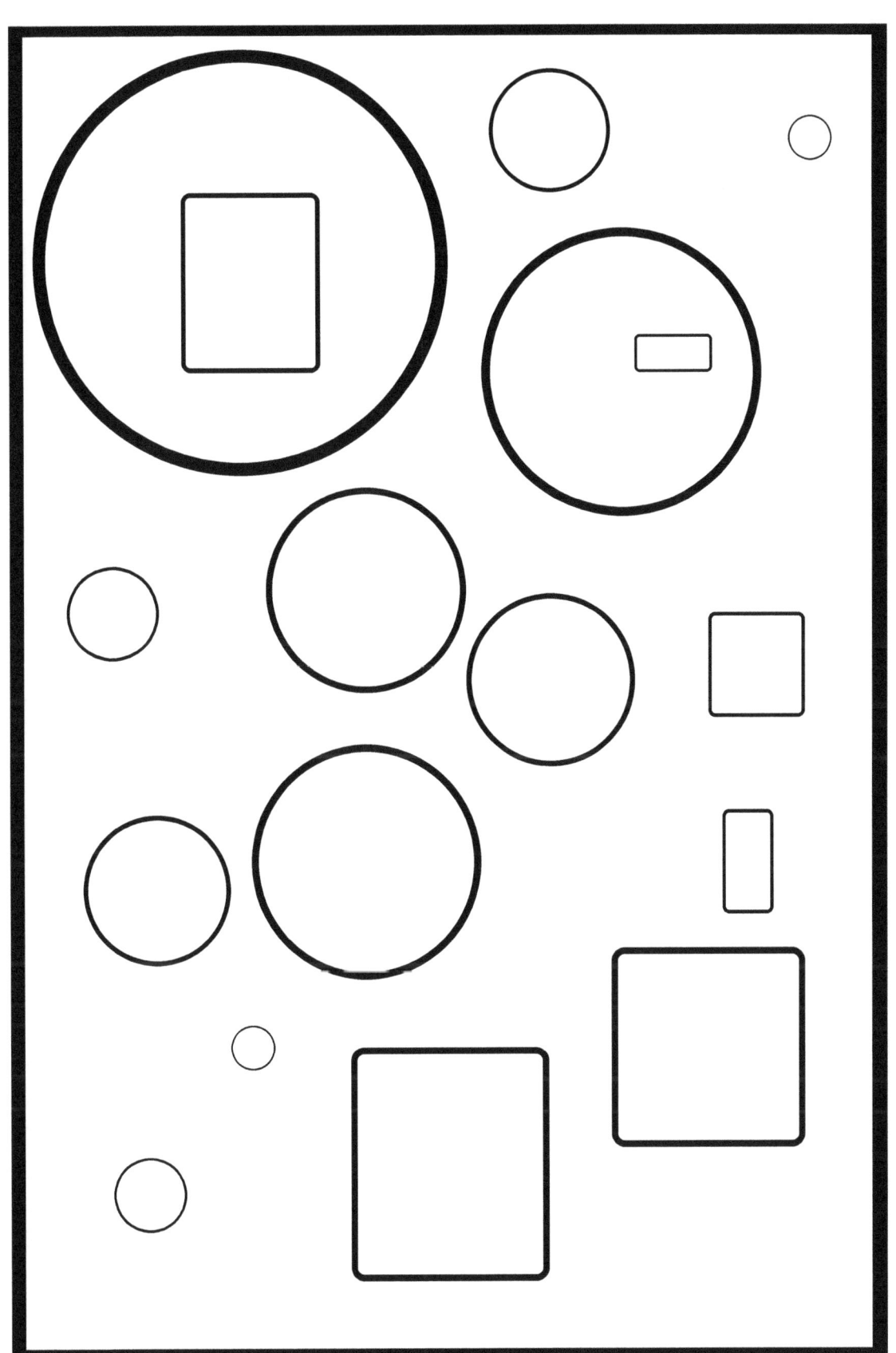

SOLUTION

FIND THE SAME SIZE

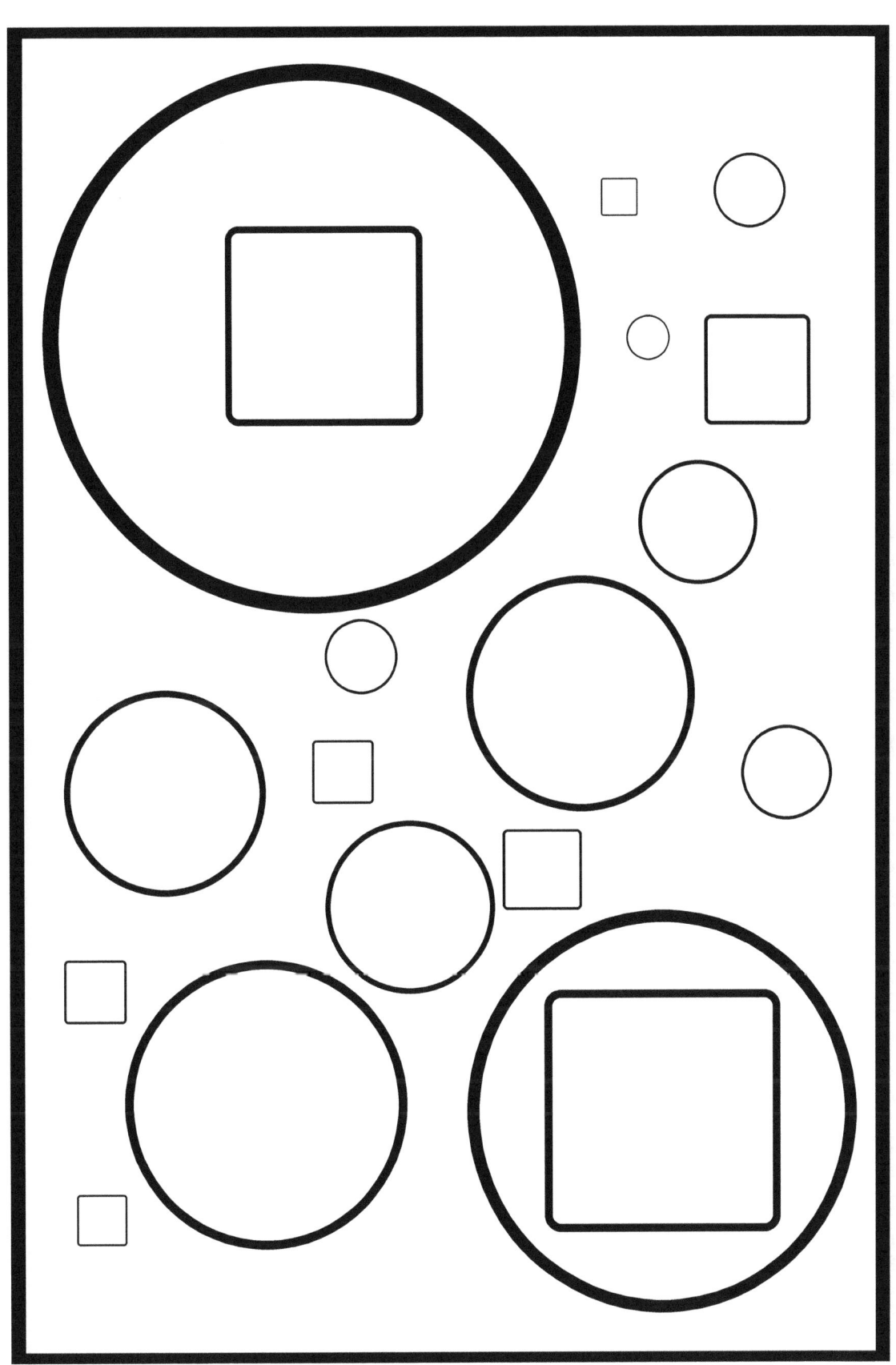

SOLUTION

FIND THE SAME SIZE

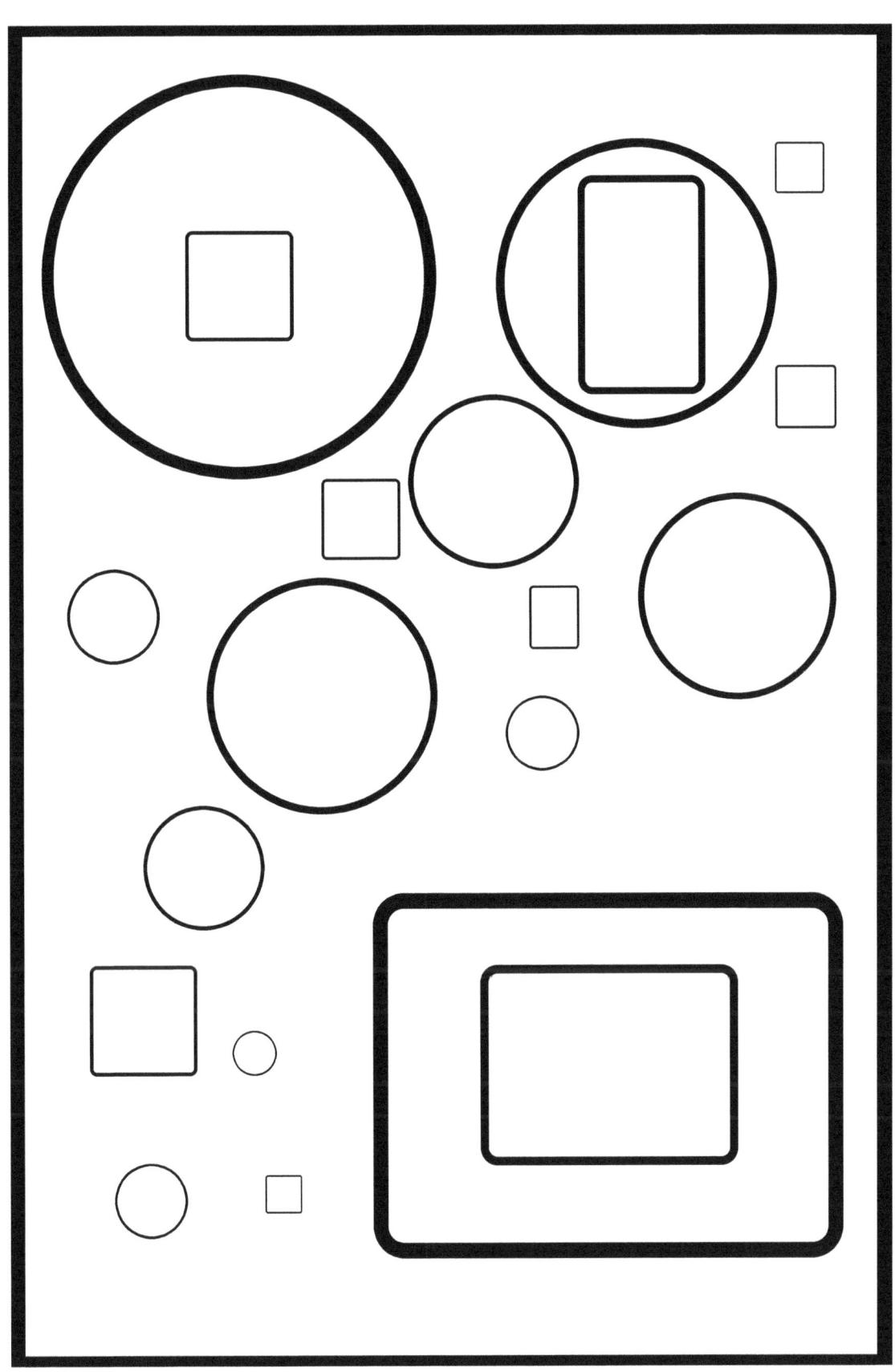

SOLUTION

FIND THE SAME SIZE

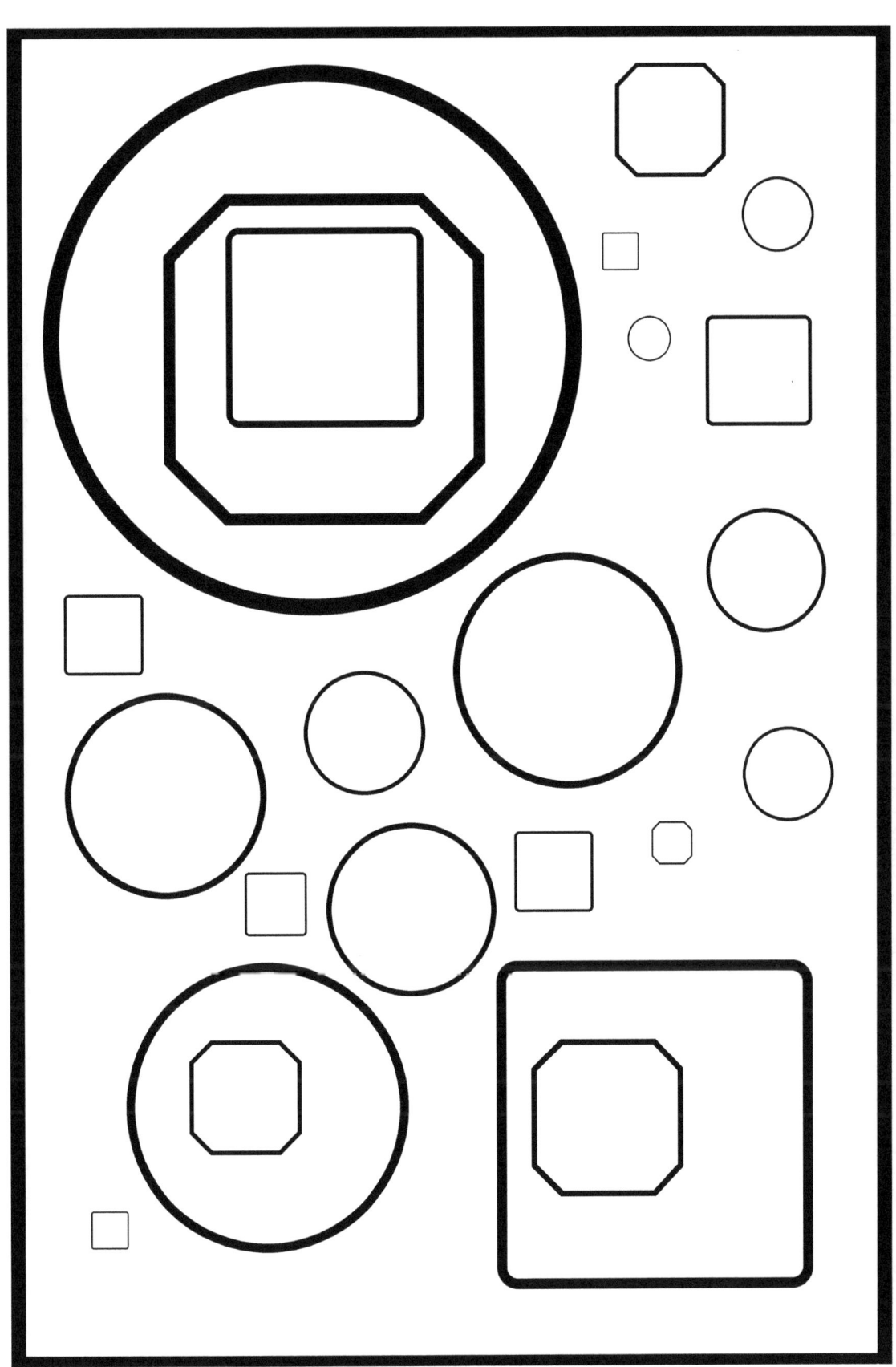

SOLUTION

FIND THE SAME SIZE

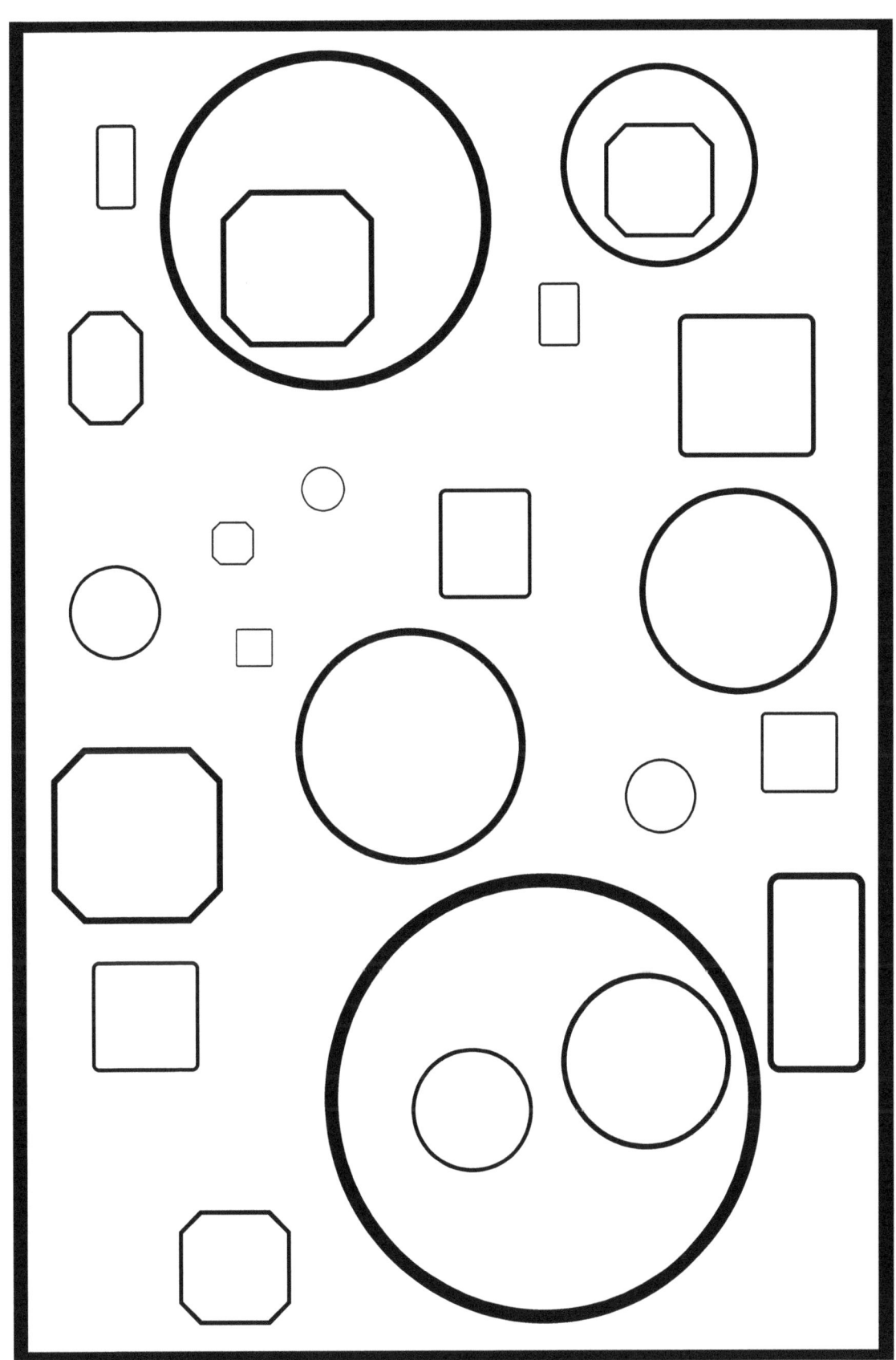

SOLUTION

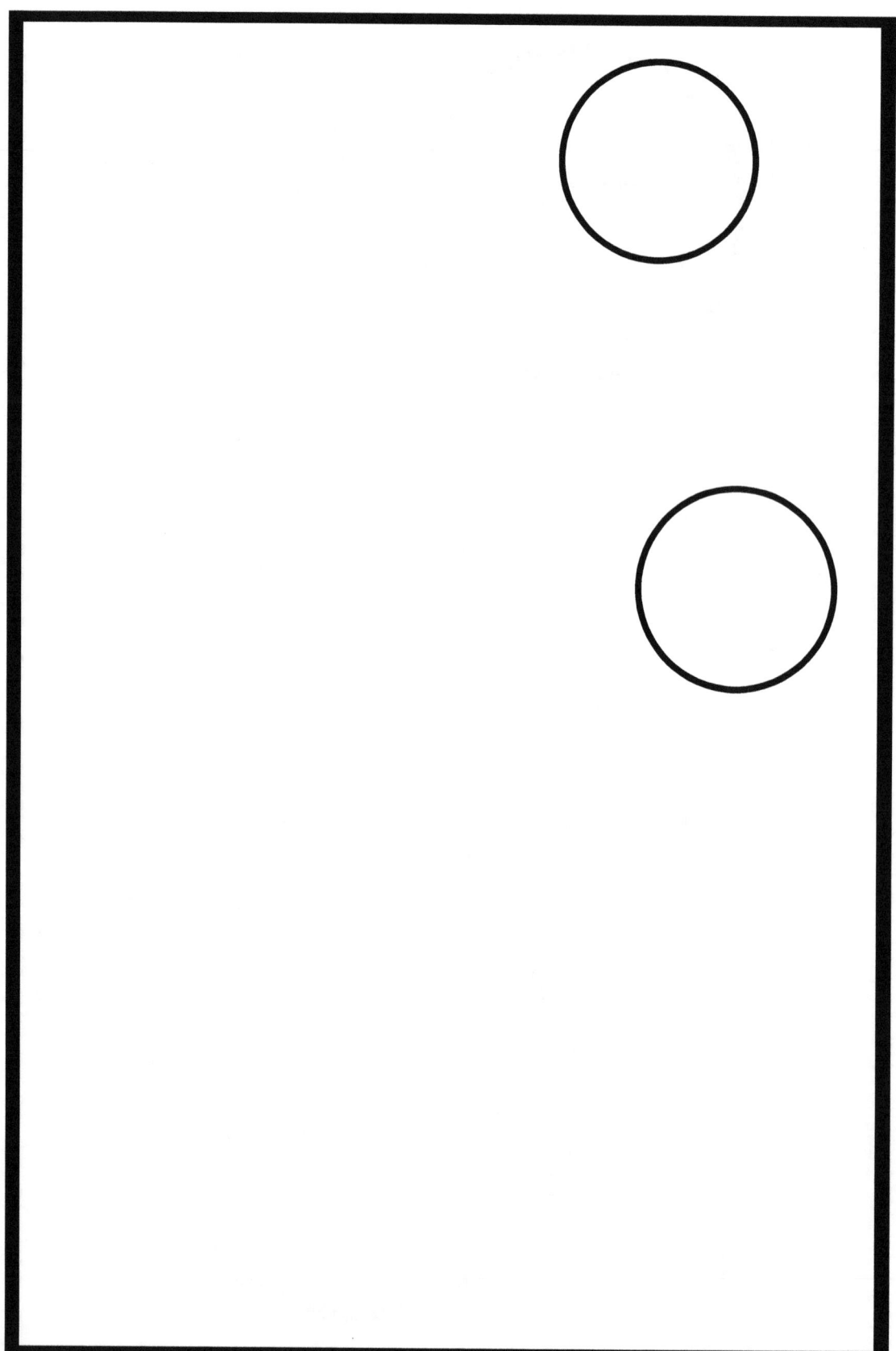

BATTLESHIP

A A A A A
B B B B
C C C
D D   D D
E   E   E

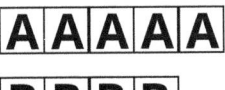

A A A A A
B B B B
C C C
D D   D D
E   E   E

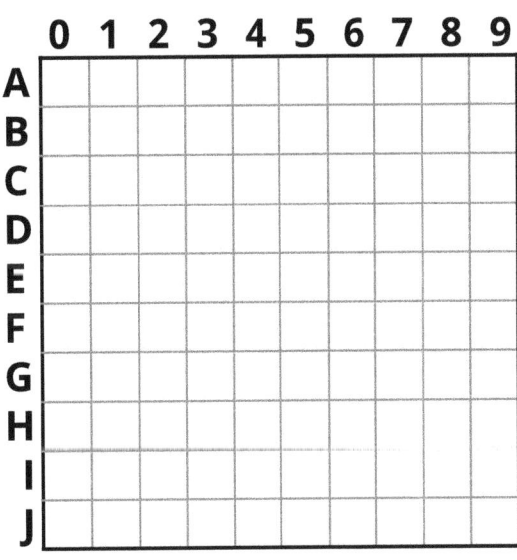

BATTLESHIP

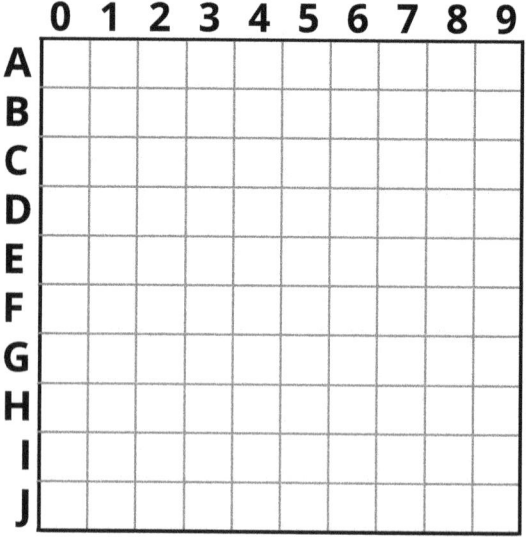

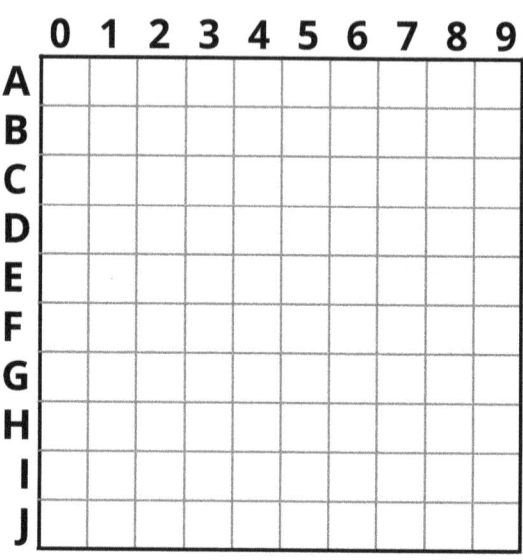

BATTLESHIP

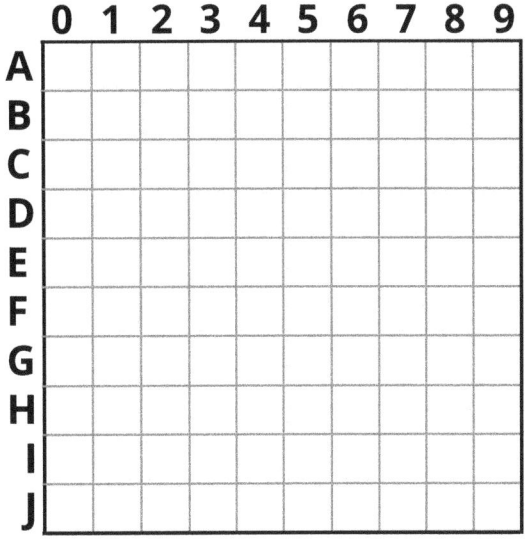

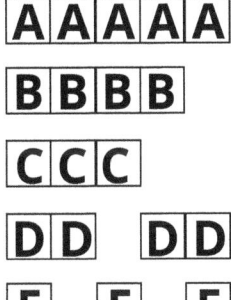

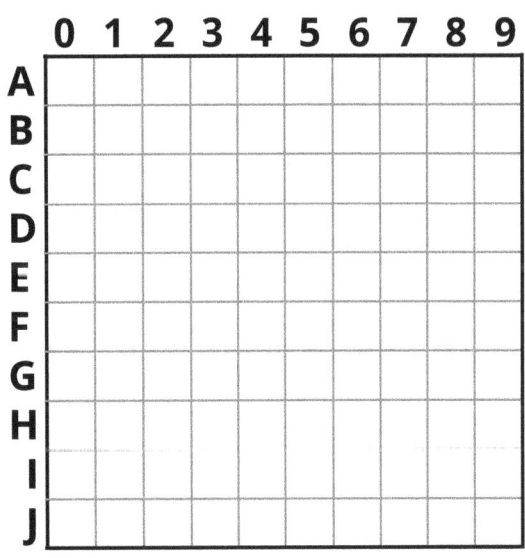

BATTLESHIP

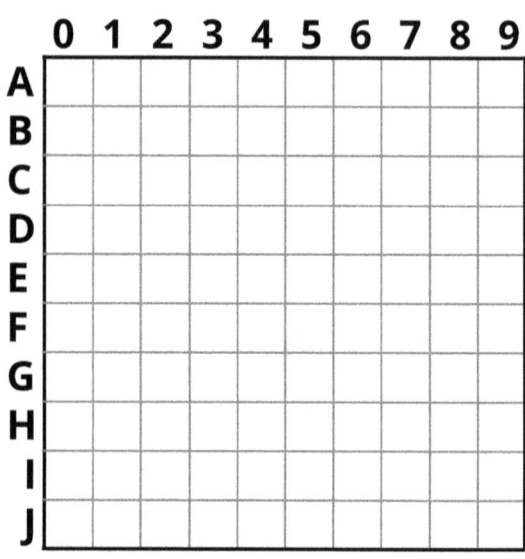

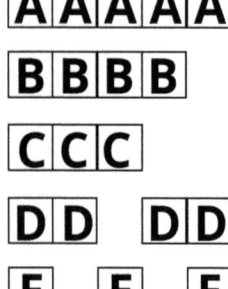

BATTLESHIP

A A A A A
B B B B
C C C
D D   D D
E   E   E

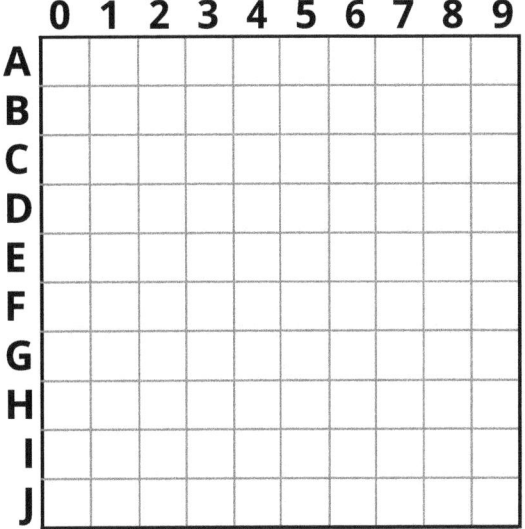

A A A A A
B B B B
C C C
D D   D D
E   E   E

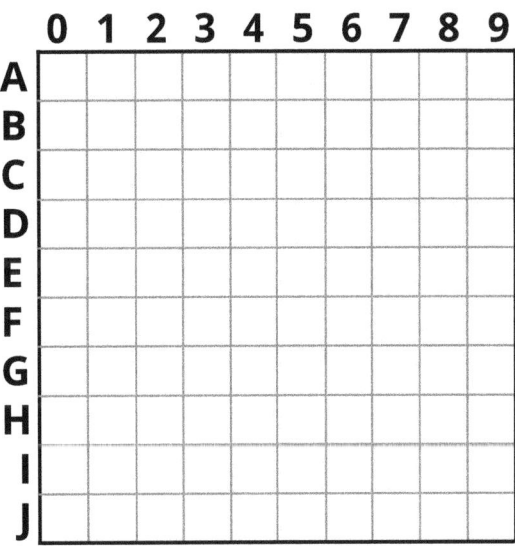

BATTLESHIP

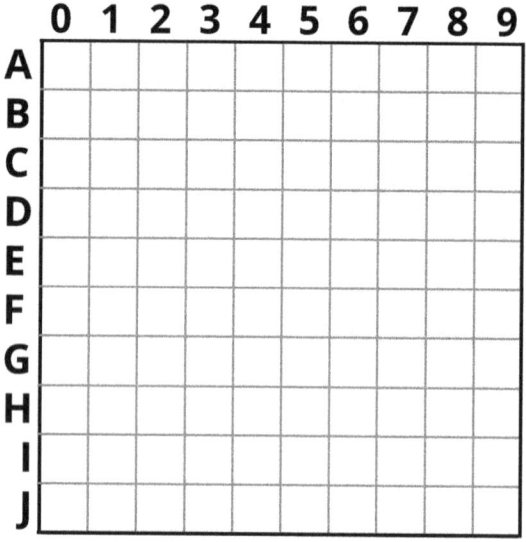

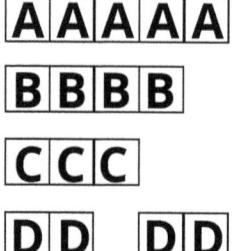

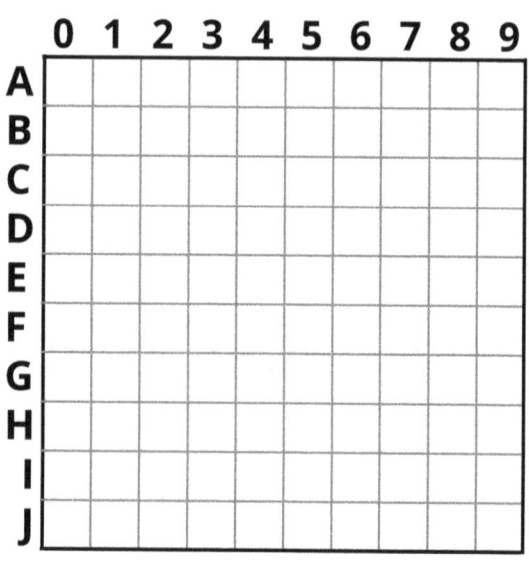

BATTLESHIP

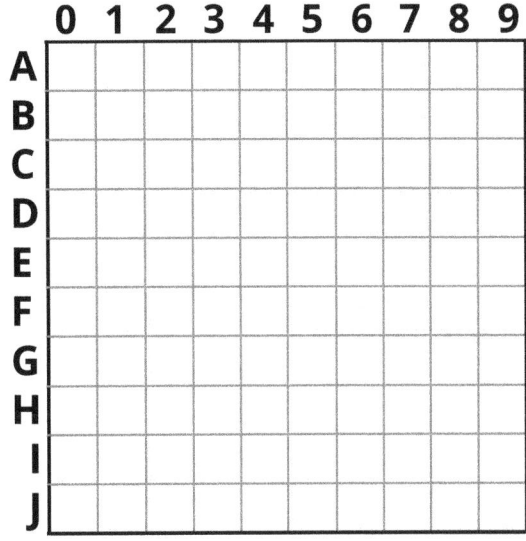

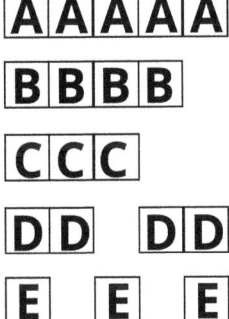

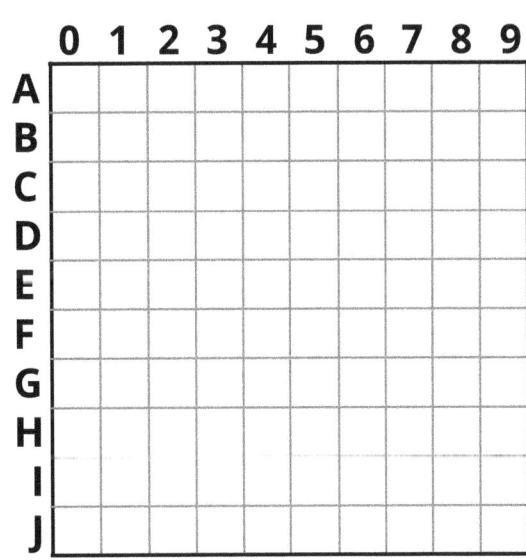

BATTLESHIP

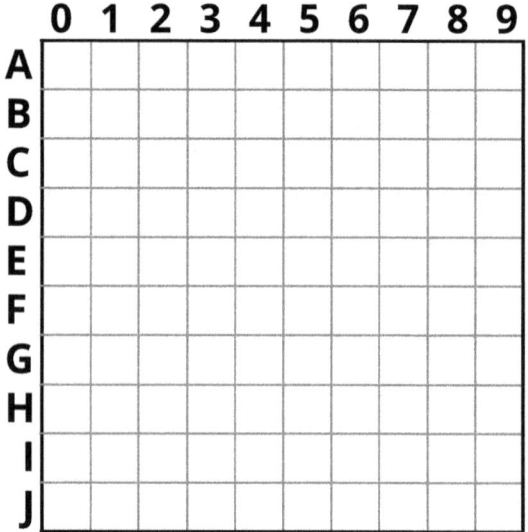

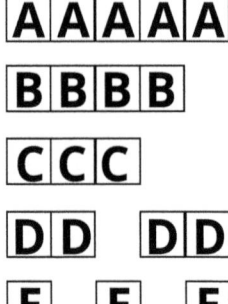

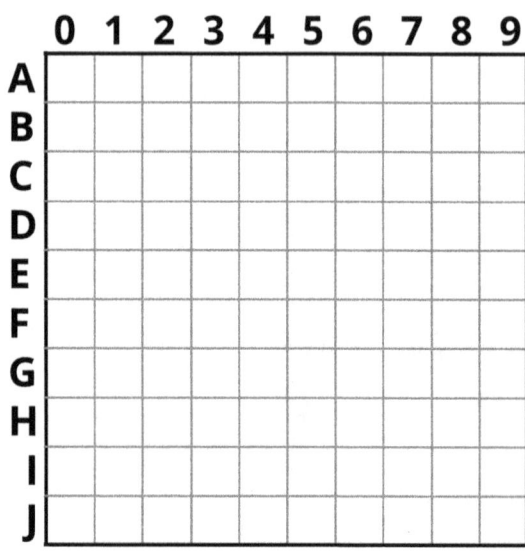

BATTLESHIP

A A A A A
B B B B
C C C
D D   D D
E   E   E

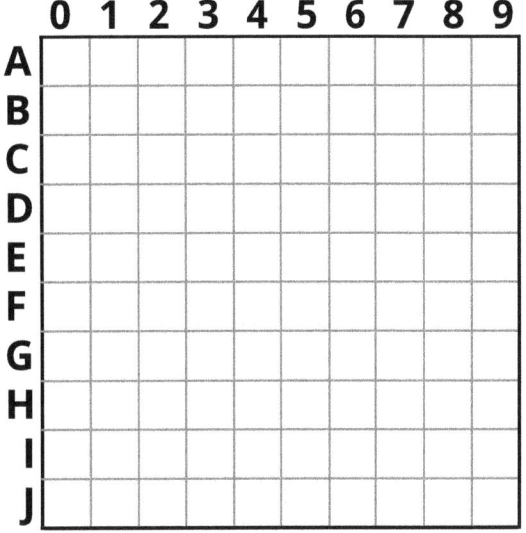

A A A A A
B B B B
C C C
D D   D D
E   E   E

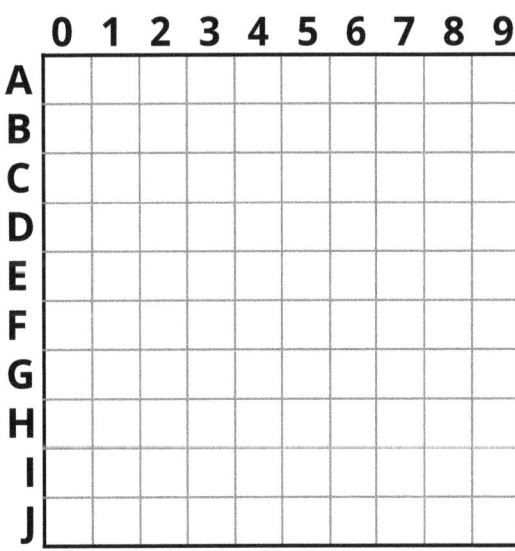

BATTLESHIP

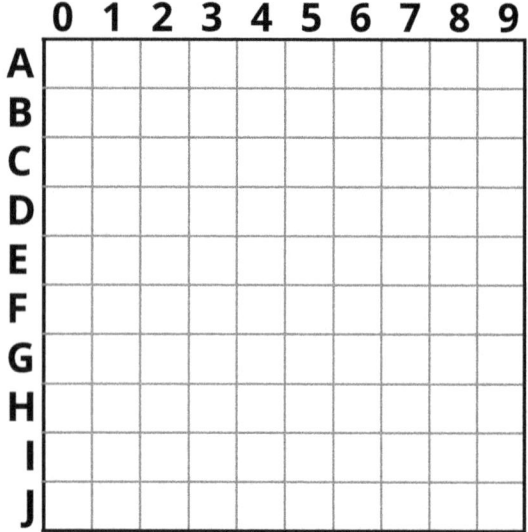

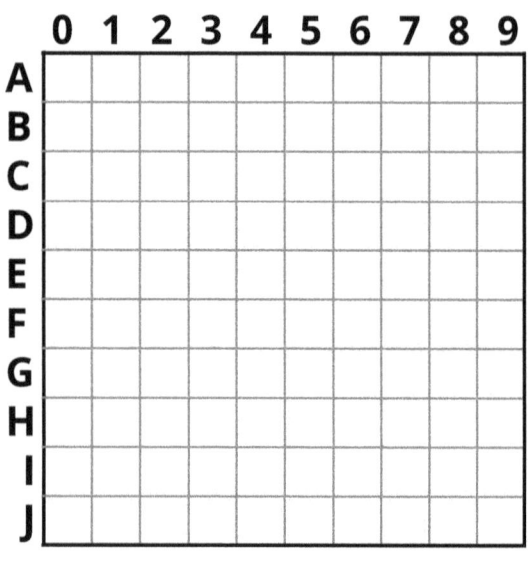

BATTLESHIP

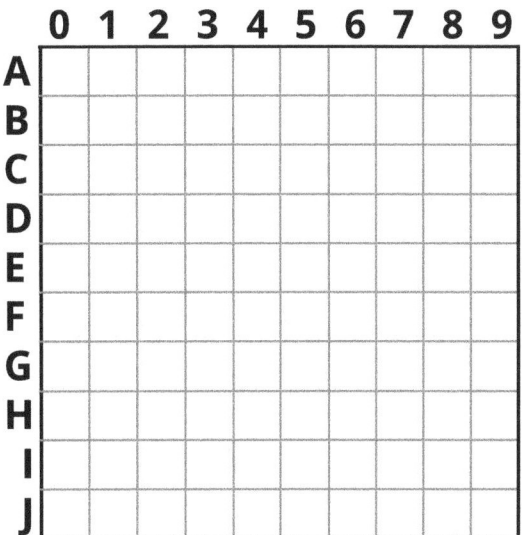

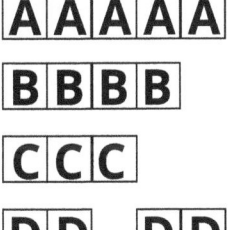

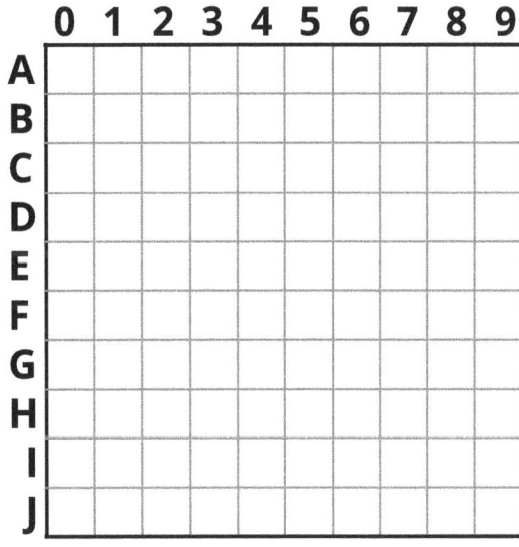

BATTLESHIP

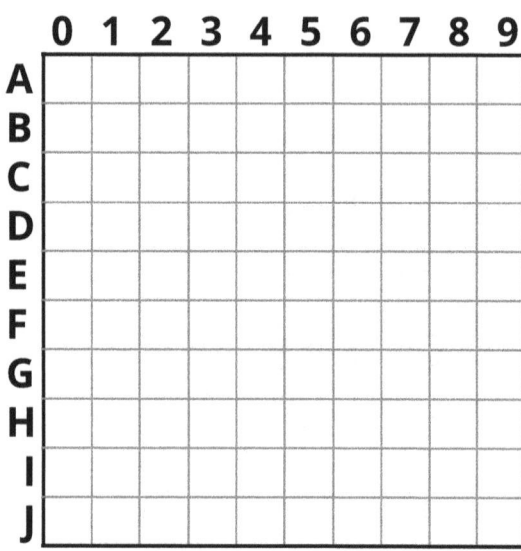

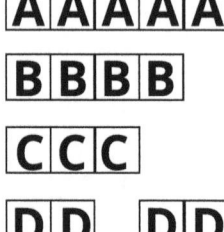

Lightning Source UK Ltd.
Milton Keynes UK
UKHW031120120620
364898UK00008B/221